SURVIVAL LEVITATION

The Little Manual That Tells You How

PATRICK L. MALLORY

BALBOA
PRESS
A DIVISION OF HAY HOUSE

Copyright © 2014 Patrick L. Mallory.

All rights reserved. No part of this book may be used or reproduced by any means, graphic, electronic, or mechanical, including photocopying, recording, taping or by any information storage retrieval system without the written permission of the publisher except in the case of brief quotations embodied in critical articles and reviews.

Balboa Press books may be ordered through booksellers or by contacting:

Balboa Press
A Division of Hay House
1663 Liberty Drive
Bloomington, IN 47403
www.balboapress.com
1 (877) 407-4847

Because of the dynamic nature of the Internet, any web addresses or links contained in this book may have changed since publication and may no longer be valid. The views expressed in this work are solely those of the author and do not necessarily reflect the views of the publisher, and the publisher hereby disclaims any responsibility for them.

The author of this book does not dispense medical advice or prescribe the use of any technique as a form of treatment for physical, emotional, or medical problems without the advice of a physician, either directly or indirectly. The intent of the author is only to offer information of a general nature to help you in your quest for emotional and spiritual well-being. In the event you use any of the information in this book for yourself, which is your constitutional right, the author and the publisher assume no responsibility for your actions.

Any people depicted in stock imagery provided by Thinkstock are models, and such images are being used for illustrative purposes only.
Certain stock imagery © Thinkstock.

Printed in the United States of America.

ISBN: 978-1-4525-2036-0 (sc)
ISBN: 978-1-4525-2037-7 (e)

Balboa Press rev. date: 9/3/2014

Few feats have captured the imagination of men and women as much as the ability to engage in unaided flight. To fly, to soar like a bird, to touch the sky, think of it—freedom from the pull of gravity.

In our not-so-distant past, if you even considered the notion that people could fly or even leave the ground for a few feet, you would have been branded a heretic or a witch or a demon in human form. You might have even been killed. The thing is, although times have changed, people have not, so it goes without saying that a small warning is in order. There is simply no reason to demonstrate levitation because people are not nearly as open-minded as you might think. The actual act of levitation frightens people and can cause heart attacks, fainting, and many other stress-related problems. If you harm someone in this way, it's the same as if you hurt him or her with a gun or a knife. Don't do it!

I would also like you to consider something else for a moment. Anything you have that will help you survive is an asset only as long as it's a secret. Let me give you an example. In the 1950s and 1960s when I was growing up, bomb shelters were all the rage. We also did duck-and-cover drills in school, which involved getting under our desks on our knees and covering our heads with our hands. Our teachers had us convinced that in the event of an actual nuclear explosion in our area, being under our desks with our little butts in the air would actually make us safer. Even in the third grade, this didn't seem logical to me somehow, but what could I do?

Let's get back to the bomb shelters. Let's say that Joe digs a hole in his backyard and installs a bomb shelter. If there is a housewife within one mile of this activity, the entire neighborhood will know everything there is to know about it within the hour. The Central Intelligence Agency has for many years tried to duplicate this level of efficiency in information gathering and as yet has failed miserably. Now what do you think will happen if there is an actual emergency and Joe decides to use his bomb shelter? You can bet that everyone in the vicinity who did not build a bomb shelter will show up demanding to use Joe's, and it doesn't matter if Joe and his family die as a result of the entire community trying to get into the shelter. When people panic, it's every man and woman for themselves.

Is there a solution to this problem? Believe it or not, shotgun sales went up dramatically during this period. That's right—people who built bomb shelters went out and bought shotguns so they could defend their bomb shelters from the panicked masses. God forbid there was ever a false alarm. How many would have died in that mess? Are you starting to see how keeping survival-related objects or abilities secret might be to your advantage?

How does my little bomb shelter story relate to levitation? Let's say you demonstrate levitation to the guys in your office. One day there's a fire that traps you and your coworkers on the tenth floor of your office building. You know levitation can save your life because you can control your rate of descent from high places with this ability, so you calmly break a window and prepare to exit this nightmare and go on about your business elsewhere.

As you leave, you notice a problem: You have acquired three new buddies you didn't even know you had, and they have a death grip around your waist, neck, and legs. They know in their panicked hearts that you will get them safely to the ground—after all, you're the guy who can actually levitate—so all four of you hit the ground at the same speed you would have if you didn't know how to levitate, killing yourself and your three new friends in one big dramatic splat. This can be really hard on new friendships!

Now let's say that you chose to keep your ability to levitate a secret instead. As you are breaking a window, you might have someone telling you not to jump and that suicide is not the answer, but you turn and tell that person that you just need air. This time when you leave the building, you leave without three friends hanging onto you. You get to the ground safely and walk up to a fireman. "Look up there on the tenth floor," you say. "There are people trapped up there." You manage to save other people's lives as well as your own. Do you know why? You kept your mouth shut. It's that simple. So I implore you—no, I beg you—if you decide to follow me down this path, let's keep it between us. You're nobody's clown; if they want a levitation demonstration, let them go through the work themselves and achieve it.

Another real interesting point is that many religions have pushed their beliefs and systems of philosophy by displaying levitation and other "magical" abilities. A group of folks come to mind who teach a form of mantra meditation; on a regular basis, they publish pictures of their practitioners several feet off the floor. I'd be willing to say that the pictures are real. If you're willing to spend the next couple of years chanting one phrase over and over and over and over, you might fly, too.

There's an interesting thing the mind does to escape monotony: It creates. Sometimes it might create thoughts, dreams, and aspirations, but if you are really doing something boring, it might create "magical" phenomena (I love the word "magic" because it's just so magical). The reason for this is plain enough—the mind loves freedom. It detests being boxed up even for a second and will do anything to escape its prison.

As much as I like to kid the meditation folks, I will say this: Meditation is a very useful tool for developing the mind's ability to concentrate and open the doors to greater mental horizons. Note the word "tool" because that is a good way to think of meditation; it is not something to be done all the time. It's time to let you in on a little secret.

Levitation is not a by-product of meditation and is not even a "magical" ability. No secret spells or magical incantations will make this thing called levitation a reality for you. It can be done and has been done by a great many people, and some will even tell you that you must be spiritually pure to achieve it. However, let me show you how that may not be true; for example, some decidedly unspiritual folks in history have had the ability to levitate.

His name was whispered in the leaves and spoken by the wind as he ran with his hand held close to the wound in his side. He did not think of the pain of the knife or the death that might follow, for there had always been pain, and death was something he had learned to accept as part of the illusion of life in the scheme of totality.

His mission was complete here. The warlord lay dead in a pool of his quickly cooling blood. All he could do now was evade his pursuers or die rather than allow capture. This was the way of his clan and the way of his grandfathers before him. This is what a Ninja knows as honor—succeed or die. So he ran until he reached the edge of a great cliff. His head turned quickly to the side so as to better hear his enemies who were giving chase and to gauge the time he had to prepare.

He knew at once his time was very short indeed, with no time to hide and not enough time to navigate the cliff face safely in the

dark. For many men, this would be the end of the hunt and a time to die. For you see, men foster illusions of what they can and cannot do, just like the fabled grass-eating tigers of Japan that believed themselves to be sheep.

The bitter wind blew against his face, but he did not notice it. He had already begun to concentrate his breathing in order to better feel the energy inside. Even as he did this, he started to untie the belt around his middle and take a firm grip on each lower corner of his night coat. He knew from discipline that he could do nothing until the energy was heightened to the point of lift, so he pushed the energy with the power of his intention and the urgency of his need. He felt the lightness and realized the soles of his shoes had begun to slip on the ground. It was time to act. He shuffled two small steps to the edge of the cliff and walked off into darkness.

To say he fell would be untrue. His body did not fall but merely coasted in the darkness, with his awareness only on the task of maintaining control of his energy. The peril of his choice had the effect of making his concentration complete. His night coat filled with air from the speed of his descent, and any fool who watched would assume the coat itself acted as a brake to slow the Ninja's fall, but this was not true. The coat only acted to stabilize his fall and to free his mind to concentrate fully on the energy. As he felt his speed slowing and the tension in the coat lessening, he pushed the energy slightly forward to change his point of landing to clear the rocks at the base of the cliff.

Time has no meaning to the mind solely intertwined with the task at hand, and a thousand eternities passed before he touched the ground. When this happened, he rolled to break his fall, but it was hardly necessary because he had no weight to his body and therefore left no impressions on the meadow beneath him.

He looked back up the cliff at his enemies who were just now coming to the cliff's edge. Two hundred and fifty feet above his head, the torches appeared like small candle flames, and there would be no illumination this far below. Still he knew he must clear out of this area for the guards might shoot arrows down the cliff face in desperation. They had already gotten lucky once at his expense, so there was no need to allow them a second chance. As he began to run once again a soft laugh escaped his lips...

This story is based in fact; only the names have been changed to protect the innocent (just kidding). I actually have no claim to secret Ninja techniques, but I have read quite a few books written by various authorities on the subject. In one of these books, there is a picture of a practitioner of Ninjutsu jumping from a high cliff holding the bottom of his night uniform, which looks like a karate uniform top but is longer.

The thing that's funny about this little fantasy is that there has to be something more to it. In almost every neighborhood in America, there's some little guy who jumps from the top of a garage with a homemade parachute. (This form of mental disease seems to affect male children mostly.) After medical treatment by Mom, Dad, or the family doctor, our hero decides to take up safer forms of play... for a while. The bottom line is that a spread-out coat is not enough to break someone's fall from any height.

As the name of this book implies, levitation can be viewed as a survival ability rather than a magical or esoteric rite. When it is necessary to walk silently on a noisy surface or to escape danger from a long way up or down, levitation can be a lifesaver. In certain disciplines, it has been used just for these types of purposes. Many Oriental martial artists today display the ability to weigh nothing while standing on a scale. Think for a moment how high you could jump if you had no weight to your body!

It is with this mind-set that I have chosen to write this manual. Also this is one of society's little (can't be done) illusions. If I achieve nothing more with this work than to start you on the road to seeing past all the illusions society has implanted in your brain, then I will have achieved a great deal indeed.

The rest of the book deals with the various things that I feel are necessary to your achieving levitation. I refuse to make this manual complicated. You bought a book on levitation, and that's what you are going to get. I will include a simple meditation for people who have a hard time with concentration (think of this section of the manual as a bonus because it is not necessary to the process of learning levitation). You might laugh at how simple my method of teaching levitation is, but you won't laugh at the results. In fact, if your initial reaction to your first levitation experience is anything like mine, it might just scare you a little bit.

Following are the titles of the book's sections:

GIVING YOURSELF PERMISSION
AN EXERCISE TO BUILD INTERNAL ENERGY
UNDERSTANDING THE MOVEMENT OF ENERGY
EXERCISES TO BUILD YOUR ABILITY TO LEVITATE
THE LEARNED ABILITY OF CONCENTRAITION
THE ABILITY TO LEVITATE (AND ALL THAT IT ENTAILS)

I suggest that you review all the information presented above before starting. With that said, let's begin.

GIVING YOURSELF PERMISSION

(How to Achieve the Impossible If Someone Only Knew It Was Possible)

I'd like to start this chapter by telling you a few of the little stories I've collected over the years. Some are well documented, and some are simply odd little articles and observations made by people in various professions. When and where they happened is not nearly as important as what I'm trying to get you to understand.

I will make no secret of what I believe in this regard. Simply stated, I believe we are *thought*. I believe everything in our outer environment is a form of thought projected so as to seem undeniably real. The most important thing I have experienced in this regard is that when we change a part of the thought that makes us and defines us, the outer environment has no choice but to adapt and change. The inner always affects the outer. It's all connected, folks.

The first story is about a little experiment that was done by psychology students back when I was a young boy. As I heard the story, it involved two groups of students; neither group played basketball as a sport. It was known that at one time or another these guys had probably played with a basketball, but the important thing was that none of them did so on a team or as a long-term form of play.

The first group was asked to practice playing basketball for about an hour a day, so for about an hour a day these guys would get together and practice playing basketball to the best of their ability. They were taught the rules of the game and how to do basic shots like layups, dunks, and jump shots as well as basic ball-handling skills.

The second group was also trained in the same way except they, unlike the first group, were not allowed to practice. They were taught to do the dunks, layups, jump shots, and basic ball-handling techniques just like the first group, but after they demonstrated a basic understanding of the techniques involved, they were no longer allowed to continue with physical basketball playing.

Instead, and this is where it gets interesting, the second group practiced in their mind. For one hour a day, they played basketball in their imagination while seated in a slightly darkened room. They had a trainer whose job it was to take them through the drills and skills that would make them an excellent team, but he was only a voice in the room. His job was to guide the visualization session; group two never physically practiced with their trainer.

This went on for a period of thirty days, if memory serves me correctly, and then a game was played between the two groups. I wish I could tell you the group that used their imagination beat the pants off the group that practiced on a court daily. This did not happen, but—and this is an amazing thing—group two did not lose that badly. They only lost by a couple of points and played a very good game.

How is this possible? How can a mental practice be transformed into physical experience? The real reason I shared this experiment with you is that I wanted you to see that something more is happening here. What is that something? The answer is simply "thought." I have to warn you, though—"thought" is not nearly as simple as you may think. In this case, thought literally replaced practice or, to put it another way, experience.

Let me give you another example of a story from my collection. It tells of a very interesting botany experiment that involved taking a fresh potato from the ground and cutting it in half. Then one half was exposed to an electrical stimulus while the other half, clear across the room, was monitored with a very sensitive sensor to see if there was a reaction. To everyone's amazement, the second half of the potato did react when the first half was given the stimulus. This continued for about twenty or so minutes until the two halves seemed to lose their oneness so to speak; after that, they reacted like two separate potatoes.

Wow, potato telepathy! Who would have thought it was possible. Considering that a potato does not have a brain as we know it, perhaps telepathy might not be what we are really seeing. Here's what I think. A potato is a slow-growing tuber, so the thought that makes and defines it must also be slow to react. What I believe we're really seeing here is a living thought in the form of a potato that takes twenty minutes to recognize it's no longer whole.

Did you know that it has been widely recognized by the scientific community that if a group of scientists believes a particular experiment is going to go a certain way, usually it will? In very sensitive experiments, thought becomes even more of a problem. This is the main reason that two different groups of highly trained and disciplined scientists researching the exact same subject many times come up with totally different answers to the same question. It would seem as though the thinking of the scientists and their attitudes can affect matter—even the very structure of reality (in this case, the outcome of an experiment).

Finally, let me share with you a personal experience rather than someone else's. I once had the opportunity to meet an old dowser. I met him when I was about fifteen years old and he must have been at least eighty. I worked at a tiny little restaurant as a busboy and lead bottle washer at the time. One of the waitresses told me that the old guy sitting in the corner was a professional dowser and that if there was water to be found, he would find it. He would also tell you, with uncanny accuracy, how deep in the ground it was.

I knew I had to seek out the secret of this man's incredible ability. So being the subtle guy I was when I was fifteen, I walked up and introduced myself, asked if I could join him, sat down, and proceeded to pepper the old guy with questions. Now I wish I could tell you he gave me the secret to dowsing, but that did not happen—or maybe it did and I'm guilty of looking for a complex answer to a simple question.

What he claimed to be the secret to dowsing for water was that the person doing the dowsing had to have a lot of electricity in his or her system. He next said that one of the ways you could tell if you had a lot of electricity in your system was if you could punch tunnels in the fog on a foggy day just by concentration alone.

I looked outside, and it was perhaps the foggiest morning I'd ever seen in that small town, so I asked him to demonstrate this ability. He chuckled and said he'd be glad to if I would just let him finish his breakfast. After finishing his meal, he led me outside and raised his arm to about shoulder level. He then exhaled and pushed his palm away from his body.

Right across the lot from this small restaurant was a gas station, and it was in this direction that a tunnel about three feet wide and growing appeared, just as he had said it would. He pushed it all the way to the bay door of the lube area, which I could see was now closed. At that point of my life, I had never witnessed a physical display of thought projection except for some minor telekinetic ability my mother had. I myself couldn't move anything with my mind, and I was awed by this man's "electrical" fog-tunneling trick.

He asked me if I would like to try, and I said sure. So I pushed my palm out and managed to punch a little tunnel in the fog myself. It was nowhere as grand as the old guy's, but it was there. I was elated. Suddenly I knew I was the most powerful fifteen-year-old in the universe. At that point, I was ready to thank all the little people who had made that moment possible. I did remember to thank the old man for showing me this awesome fog-punching ability, so in my elation I did not make a complete fool of myself.

Then something odd happened. I noticed the next day as I stood outside my home on an equally foggy morning, before I went to work, that I could not even make a dent in the fog. Not a wrinkle appeared before my eyes as I pushed with all my mental might. How could this be? Was it that my mighty mental fog-punching ability had somehow been worn out? Was I tired?

When I got to work that morning at the restaurant, I tried again. It was as foggy as the previous day, and when I stood where the old man had stood, I again could punch a small hole through the fog. I realized that after some experimentation, I didn't have this ability myself but in fact had only borrowed this awesome fog-tunneling feat from the old dowser himself.

One other thing I must share with you is that the only way I could make this work was if I stood where he had stood. You see, it was as if the area he had stood on had somehow changed. The reality was slightly different in this area. The laws that governed that little patch of ground didn't quite match up with those of its surroundings. I noticed that this continued for about three days. On each day, it got progressively weaker; finally on the fourth day, I couldn't make the fog move at all. It was as if the reality of the area had once again settled back to what it was before all this had started.

You might ask what I learned. The answer is that thought, or at least a heightened ability that is controlled by thought, can be borrowed. I've heard several stories from people who have had the opportunity to be around a strong psychic and have noted how much more intuitive they seemed to be while in the person's presence. Some even believe they've been permanently altered by this contact, and who knows, maybe they have.

I'd like you to note that thought expressed with intense concentration (or in this case, with power behind it) can alter the reality of a given area for a time. I'd like you to ask yourself a question: If thought and reality are so different, how can this be so? How can thought literally change the way a place manifests itself? A haunted house is a variation on this theme. It's not that there's a ghost causing the problems but rather that the house in question has been imprinted with a horrible and very emotional thought event, and this event is literally played over and over again like a tape that the house just can't shake.

You're probably wondering why I'm sharing these strange little stories with you. Well, there's a method to my madness, I assure you. Let's recap the brief examples that I've shared with you:

- **Thought can replace experience, as it did for the basketball players.**
- **Thought doesn't seem to recognize the boundaries of space, as was seen in the potato experiment.**
- **Thought can change the outcome of something you attempt based on how you believe it will come out, as many scientists can attest.**
- **Thought can be borrowed and can even change the fabric of reality in a given area for a time, as I personally experienced with the old dowser in front of a little diner.**

I have many more of these types of stories in my collection and could probably fill a book with them, but that's not what this manual is about. What I am trying to get you to see is that thought is not just the noise inside your head. Yes, that's one form of thought, but there are many others. What thought isn't is a limitation, unless you set limits on it. Then those limits are as powerful as you make them. Personally I believe that everything is thought or an expression of thought, as I stated earlier.

During your whole life, you have been conditioned to believe that it's your environment that has made you who you are. That being said, let me ask you this: Have you ever thought that maybe your environment might be a product of your thought as well as you being a product of your environment? I mean maybe, just maybe, your thought might have just as big an impact on your environment as it has on you. Please don't get me wrong; I don't mean you've created the entire world, but think of how many things in your life have come into being because you thought they should.

If we look back to the sixteenth century, we meet a philosopher by the name of René Descartes, who was considered by many to be the father of rational philosophy. Plainly stated, René Descartes and many like him believed that the thought inside your head and the reality outside your body were two totally different things. This philosophy reduced the concept of thought applied to reality to mere childish daydreams.

So began the age of skepticism, and the fledgling material sciences of the time began their ascent to our present day. On the plus side, many of our superstitions go by the wayside in this new age of rationality, but I have to ask at what price. We've come to the point in our thinking that if there is not a rational explanation for something, we simply choose not to believe its viability. Believe me, this is a sad, small type of thinking, a type of thinking which does not promote levitation or any other so-called psychic ability.

When you start to see that the primary reason for this type of thinking is actually philosophical, perhaps you will grow past it. When you start to see that thought is actually a much bigger part of the picture of life than you have previously allowed, you can and will use thought to control many of the things you believed you were helpless against.

I'm going to share a technique with you that will allow you to change your thought. Notice that I am not talking about changing your beliefs because beliefs have nothing to do with reality but rather are something your mind uses to shape its judgment of what it senses. Without beliefs or preconceived ideas, your mind would only observe and not judge its reality; that might sound good, but in reality you need to judge everything you encounter because—let's face it—this world has teeth and a misjudgment can leave you badly bitten.

Also, beliefs do not institute action. You probably already believe levitation is possible or you would not have bought this book. Your belief will not get you off the floor, but when you change the thought that makes and defines you, then and only then will you realize the reality of levitation. I guess the best way I can say it is this: When you change your beliefs, many times you will change your perspective. You will see things in a different light so to speak, but this (in and of itself) does not change what you can do.

When you change your thought, you change yourself; in so doing, you affect your inner mental environment and your external environment. This can't be avoided because thought is connected to all things, both inner and outer. Do you want to know a little secret? The mind already recognizes the tremendous power in thought and knows it can affect your inner and outer environments. The way it defends against this effect is by keeping you scatterbrained, with all kinds of thoughts all over the place. Even a concentrated mind does this—it's just that the range of thoughts is more centered on the task at hand.

This is literally the way your mind tries to stabilize the thought construct that makes you who you are and what your place in reality is. Remember when I told you earlier that the mind does everything for a reason? When you start to see that you are not as separate from your environment as you've been taught but rather are an active creator of your own individual reality, you can spot many natural defenses that are built right into your mental construct.

Enough with the theory—let's move into the technique that facilitates the changes. I call this simply the "Foundation Technique." It is a very powerful technique and is one of the only techniques I know that asks you to use your fear to further your goal. You don't have to have one iota of visualization ability to use it. It also uses one of the oldest methods of teaching known—the story. While there are many exercises that will strengthen a psychic ability that already exists, with this technique you can create an ability that you have no knowledge of. You only have to know what you want the ability to do.

Let me give you an example of what I mean. When I was in the Navy, I decided to take a martial art called Kempo Karate. The only major problem I had was that I'm very nearsighted and have blind spots in my eyes due to a disease that I contracted during my childhood. In Kempo, the practitioners move very fast, so I kept getting hit because I could not see well enough to avoid that kind of speed. The first couple of months were horrible, and some of the higher-ranking students started calling me "Ever Last," which is one of the name brands of punching bags in our fair country.

About this time, I read an account of a master who managed to speed up his mind so that his opponents appeared to move in slow motion. The story itself was fictional, but the ability of the mind to speed itself up is well documented in driving. Your mind automatically speeds up when you are driving on the freeway at high speed, and when you leave the freeway, you will usually feel as if you're going really slowly for the first couple of blocks until your mind slows down and everything normalizes. This is why traffic cops sit a block or so from freeway off-ramps; it's a great way to fill their speeding ticket quotas.

Using my Foundation Technique, I made learning how to control my mind's ability to speed up my goal. For about the first thirty days, I did not notice any change and kept getting hit religiously. Then something happened, and I started to get control of it. I don't know how and can't describe what magic mind muscles to flex, but I started to be able to speed my mind up slightly. I will not tell you it was as if the other students were going in slow motion, but it was as if they were going at a normal speed, a speed I could easily deal with.

The only problem I noticed with speeding up my mind was a general sense of fatigue and a dull ache in the back of my head. It was as if I had used more brain food, but I found that eating some sugar helped get me back to normal. That was the only real downside to gaining this control.

Now I was able to block, counter, and even anticipate the movements of my fellow Kempo practitioners, all because I could slightly speed up my sense of time. I quit Kempo shortly afterwards, but my point is that I had no knowledge of how to speed up my mind—I only knew I wanted to have this ability. That's what I mean when I say you can bring out an ability you have no knowledge of having. With my Foundation Technique, you only have to be able to clearly know in your mind what you want to do; then your mind's thought connection with your internal and external reality will make it happen.

As I stated earlier, the Foundation Technique does not require visualization as such but rather needs to have a story told to the practitioner. All of you who think visualization is impossible can still use this technique because it's as easy as listening to a story, so take heart. What this technique is *not* is a rehash of New Age "fluff bunny" nonsense, and there are no pink clouds or warm fuzzy feelings in this method. We will leave that nonsense to the New Age folks who just love to be amazed at someone else's ability but rarely ever accomplish anything on their own.

The Foundation Technique: Its Concepts and Explanations

Concept one: You must use your survival instincts in all of your mental conditioning!

Let's talk about the downside of your first levitation experience. Levitation shock is very real, which means that when you first achieve levitation, it usually gives you a thrill but also scares you very badly at the same time. The ability to levitate is not something most of us are prepared to accept, and many people will not try to levitate again after their first success with it. You see, when you bring a change like levitation into your life, you're challenging something much deeper than the simple ability to levitate.

You are challenging your basic survival program, the old "I must stay alive at all costs program." Levitation messes with this program in a major way simply because it changes so many preconceived notions you hold near and dear. I'd like to give you an example of how strong some of the simple little things you learned in the past can be. Here is another one of my little collected stories.

There was once a group of psychology students who made up a simple little experiment to see if people could overcome basic childhood conditioning. They got a group of adults together in a large room and gave them plenty of water, pop, ice tea, etc. The idea was for everyone to have to pee. Yes, that's right. They wanted all these adults to really want to urinate badly. Now it gets interesting.

The psychology students lined everybody up and told them to pee their pants, yes you read that correctly, to stand there and pee their pants. That's all they asked of their volunteers. I believe they even promised extra money to those who could actually do the dirty deed. Sounds pretty simple, doesn't it? It's something a child could do without hardly trying. Guess what? Most of the adults could not do it.

They really tried, but it was simply not possible because a little notion that was stuck in their head—"You don't pee your pants"—stopped them cold. Now if this wee bit of childhood conditioning had so much power over them that they chose to burst their bladder rather than violate their conditioning, how much more will learning to fly encroach on old mental notions?

Your survival instinct is so much a part of your decision-making process that you don't even see it for what it is. Levitation is something your survival instinct sees as a radical change, and radical change is not something that your survival instinct likes to see. Radical change induces uncertain outcomes that can threaten survival, which is why you will naturally find yourself fighting against any such change in yourself and your environment.

You see, folks, your survival instinct is one of the strongest programs your mind contains. It's like butting heads with a Billy Goat. You may be able to force it to change sometimes, but wouldn't it be easier if you allowed it to work with you in the process of change? When you understand this extremely important point, you can start to use your survival instinct to help bring about radical change in your life and stop beating your head against it.

This is actually easier said than done because so many methods of meditation, visualization, self-dialog, etc., don't even touch your survival instinct; instead, they ask you to relax and get warm. While you're at it, why not just go to sleep! You might as well go to sleep for all the help these methods will bring into your life. I want you to feel something intense; I want a little fear and some anxiety. I don't even care if you try to relax because we are going to bring about some serious changes, and that means work, not sleep.

So here's a question: What really scares you? For me, it's a big bear. I hate running into them in the woods, and I even have dreams of them chasing me. For you, it may be a pack of wild dogs or a gang of rough kids armed with guns and knives. Whatever it is, that's what your mind sees as a threat to your survival. In the Foundation Technique of mental programming, we are going to use this fear to our advantage. Levitation can help you escape from danger (that's why I chose to name this manual Survival Levitation). It is survival ability and nothing more.

In my case, I visualize a big, mean bear chasing me, and I use my levitation ability to quickly zip up the side of a cliff or climb a tree. It's great to get away from this animal, and I have fun visualizing his frustration at the base of the cliff or tree. Let me give you an example of what I'm teaching you.

I've been walking these woods for many years now, and if I had to choose one thing I like the most, it's the smell—the earth is so alive, moist, and fresh. The sunlight stabs through the trees here and there; where it touches, it is as if an explosion of color springs forth from the forest that otherwise looks so calm and cool in comparison. I stop for a moment and gently caress a pine branch just to feel its prickly nature. I do this in an attempt to hold this place of beauty with my sense of touch as well as sight.

An odd smell comes to my attention. It smells like a wet dog, but more intense. I look to my right, and suddenly my heart skips a beat. Standing not fifty feet away is the biggest, meanest-looking bear I've ever seen. I also realize, much to my horror, it's a she bear with cubs. No animal is more dangerous than a female bear with cubs. To understand what I mean, all you have to do is picture yourself fighting a compact car with teeth, claws, and a real bad attitude—to be honest, you'd stand a better chance with the compact car.

I start to ease away because I know running is not a good idea. I look back only to find she does not care that I'm moving slowly away. She is starting to give chase, so I now know running is indeed

my best possible idea—it's that or change my name to Purina Bear Chow. As I start to run, I have a cold, hard feeling of dread in the pit of my stomach for I know a bear can run much faster than a man. It is this dread and fear that turn on my adrenaline, and I run much faster than even I know I can. Feet don't fail me now, I silently pray.

I don't need to turn to know she has indeed closed the gap, so I choose to make a sudden right turn and fight my way through the thick brush. In my mind, I believe that she might have a harder time pursuing me as I weave my way through the trees, over logs, and around bushy areas—at least that's the plan. The first possible shortfall to my scheme happens right after I break through the bushes that line the side of this trail. I start to tumble because now I'm on a steep hillside I didn't even realize was there.

When I finally come to a stop with a bone-crunching splat, I find I'm lying on a logging road. From the sounds coming down the hill, I know I have to get moving *now*. I start to move, only to find my leg is stiff and very painful. I continue on with a limping but fast walk, only hoping that my body will not fail me now. What's important is to live through the next minutes, find a way out, get to some shelter, or hope the mama bear gives up. Desperation starts to really take hold of my heart, and for the first time I feel I may not live to see the next sunrise.

Let's stop there for a moment and look at what the story has created so far. To put it mildly, the main character is in a bad way. In the Foundation Technique, this is where I want you to feel fear, desperation, and an impending sense of doom. Just don't listen to the story unfold; be an actor who really *feels* the emotions of the play that you are in. This is why so many actors can make emotions seem so real because they really feel them! This brings us to the next important concept.

Survival Levitation

Concept two: You must be an active player in your story. You must participate emotionally and physically in your story as it unfolds.

Let me explain what I mean by "participate." One of the most important things that I want you to do in this method is feel. The true secret of the Foundation Technique's success is that you try to feel every part of it. Notice I didn't say visualize it as if you were there or really listen to the story; I said to feel the emotions. You must live and breathe them and allow yourself to be caught up in the feelings that the story you are using presents to you. Throughout the teaching of this technique, I will remind you to feel; feeling and emotion are very important and are key to making this technique work.

To give you an idea of what I'm getting at, I want you to learn something from a child. I know that it's been awhile and you're past all that, but believe me a child can remind you of so much that you have forgotten. Just watch a small boy play with his trucks or a little girl play with her doll and tea set. Notice, if you will, that the boy is not just pushing his trucks from one place to another; he's making the sounds of acceleration and braking, and if there is an accident, you will hear every bang, crash, and POW until the crash is over.

The same is true of the girl. She is really talking to the people at her tea party as if they really do exist; if you listen, you'll know what each invisible person likes in her tea, what her mood is, how she is dressed, etc. If you really look closely, you'll realize that children really don't know how to totally separate themselves from the story that they are creating in their imagination. It is through these stories that children create the thought constructs that will later define them as adult human beings.

This is what I mean when I say to feel the story you are using. If you are running in your story, breathe faster and pump your arms a little. If you turn your head in the story, slightly turn your head. If there is a reason to feel fear, then really try to feel it. The same is true of happiness or any other emotion in the story you're using—get into it! Really get into it! Even if you have to pretend, that's all right because that is the difference between a story you're listening to and a story you're living.

I continue in my limping but fast walk around a sharp bend only to find that I have come to a dead end. Around me on all sides are sheer dirt walls about fifty feet high that are wet. I can see rocks here and there, but there is nothing I can use to climb out of this gravel pit or whatever it is. I only have one choice: to go back the way I came.

As I turn around, I see that is going to be a major problem. At the entrance of my unwelcome cul-de-sac is my new best friend, the she bear from hell. Her head is bobbing back and forth, and I can see she is watching me as well as smelling the air. I have a sick feeling that she knows I'm trapped. I reach back to get a pocketknife that I keep in my back pocket and realize that even that small hope is not available because I must have lost it in the fall. I realize now that I'm going to die.

Remember I told you to use your survival instinct in your thought programming. Right about now you have your survival program's absolute attention. Why? Because you have created an unbeatable scenario, and your survival program hates unbeatable situations and will try anything just to escape. This is what panic is really about; it's your survival instinct's way of overriding thought and reason so that you might find a way that works and that saves your life.

At this point, you should try to feel the total panic and dread of the story's character. Don't be afraid of putting pauses in your story so you can really get a grip on the emotion. Really try to feel it. The next part of the story is the odd answer you are looking for, and it brings us to concept three.

Concept three: The answer (levitation) in your story must be seen as if it has already been completely mastered. You must never let the steps leading up to its achievement become a part of the story.

This is an important point in the way the mind works: The mind will give you exactly what you ask it to give you. If you talk about procedures to reach the goal, that's what your mind will give you—procedures. The goal itself can't be reached because that would mean the procedures to the goal would have to stop. It's like walking in the woods and concentrating so hard on the trail that you pass the cabin that you intended to go to. This is why I say you must not allow the procedures to the goal to become part of the story; always stick to the end result, and let the way to the goal take care of itself.

The mind is very literal, which is the real reason hypnotism often fails. The problem you're trying to overcome is mentioned, and the procedures for its solution are gone over several times in the session. Sounds good, right? However, your very literal mind gives exactly what it's asked for—the problem and the procedures—so how can your very literal mind ever get to the solution when it's tied up in the problem itself? That's why when we introduce levitation as the solution in our story, we must see it as totally mastered.

The bear comes toward me, her head moving slowly from side to side. I back up, and as I come to the end of my journey, a funny thought enters my head. At home I have completely mastered levitation. I can rise at least a foot off the floor and hold myself in position. I've never gone higher than that, but if I can go that high, what if I jumped just when I started to rise? I look behind me even though everything in me screams not to take my eyes off the bear.

The cliff is at least fifty feet above me, and I could touch it in two steps. I look back and the bear has closed the gap even more; there is no more than twenty-five feet between us. I become silent inside as I lower myself into a squatting position. The fear has tightened

my lower stomach and groin, a feeling I haven't felt since I was kid and did some of the stupid things a child does. Although there seems to be a slight sexual side effect to fear this intense, I can't say I've missed the feeling at all. I force myself to slow my breathing as my fingertips touch the rough soil between my feet. Now I look death right in the eye, and I can tell she knows she has won.

With intent born of desperation, I begin to push the energy up and slightly back (because I am leaning forward). I don't want to jump forward but rather back and up, away from the danger. She takes a step forward and lowers her head. My God, how has she gotten so close? I can't lose my concentration or surely I will die. I can really feel the energy pressing up and through my back and shoulders. Suddenly it happens; I feel myself slip slightly on the ground. There is an odd feeling of being disconnected from the very earth I stand on, so I jump up as quick and as hard as I can.

I push the energy up and slightly back even as I leave the ground. The air explodes from my lungs with force, which I know will help me to extend my energy even more. Because I know that energy will follow intent, I look up at the sky and not at the ground below my feet. Because I am looking up at the sky and have no real sense of how high I am, it surprises me to feel the sharp sting of pine needles cutting into the backs of my legs.

I look down and realize I've sailed higher than the edge of the cliff. The small pines are no more than six feet tall, and I find myself moving backwards through their upper branches. Looking down and suddenly realizing my success at gaining this height, I start to relax and now move toward the earth as my energy stabilizes. I slide gently down into a small gap between two of the pines near the edge of the cliff. As my feet touch the springy earth at the edge of the cliff, I see a large brown shape suddenly dart up the cliff face toward me. It looks for a moment as if she will make it to where I stand, so powerful is her energy in this attempt to breach this earthen barrier. Then, finding no foothold, she falls and slides, digging in all the way down to where she started at the base of the cliff. Twice more she makes the attempt to reach me and kill me, and as I watch, twice more she fails.

Probably sounds like a good place to conclude this little nightmare, but there's one more concept that must end every Foundation Technique story. You must give thanks. You must take a moment and thank your lucky stars that you learned levitation. Close your eyes and realize that if you had not completely mastered the ability to levitate, you would now be dead or severely injured. There is a very powerful secret to this type of story ending in Foundation Technique.

Concept four: You must create in your story a moment where you are thankful for the ability (levitation) that you have mastered. It should be thankfulness that you are still alive because of your mastered ability.

Are you curious as to why you must give thanks? Let me ask you something: Have you ever given thanks for something you have not received? Even if you have not had one hint that you will ever levitate, give thanks and it will happen. Thought does not recognize time; thought does not recognize sequence. If you are truly thankful for something you have received, thought does not care that it's going to happen in the future. It will happen, so the thought construct that you are will change to allow for it.

I realize now, after all that I've been through, that I hurt in more places than I can count. My lungs are tired and my heart hurts. There is an odd sense of giddiness and dizziness about me. I'm in shock to be sure, but I'm alive. When I first mastered the ability to levitate, never once did I really believe it would save my life. Now it has.

As I place my hand on my chest and feel the air that I now take into my lungs expand my chest, I feel a sense of supreme thankfulness.

I am so very thankful that I took the time to learn levitation. Most of all, I'm glad to be alive because of my ability to levitate. As I breathe out for what feels like the first time in hours, I watch the fuzzy brown backside of death lumber away and go back to her cubs and realize it's going to be all right. It is as if the universe agrees with me because the sun suddenly comes out from behind a cloud and I am bathed in light, the light of life.

All right then, let's recap. The story you use for the Foundation Technique must follow these four simple concepts.

Concept one: You must use your survival instinct in all of your mental conditioning!

Remember, folks, this is the big one. The story has to be dangerous to us; otherwise, we are doing glorified relaxation exercises. Use your fear, and make it part of your solution.

Concept two: You must be an active player in your story. You must participate emotionally and physically in your story as it unfolds.

Unlike with hypnotism, we don't get all relaxed and we don't lie down; we remain in an upright position, usually seated. If you're being chased, breathe faster and pump your arms. When you look over your shoulder in the story, make sure you turn your head slightly to coincide with what's happening in the story, which will help you really get into your story. The Foundation Technique is not a casual listening experience—you have to live it, be there, and feel it with intensity.

Concept three: The answer (levitation) in your story must be seen as if it has already been completely mastered. You must never let the steps leading up to its achievement become a part of the story.

Remember that the mind is very literal. The exercises I give in a later chapter will help you learn to control the movement of energy in the body. If you make the mistake of making these exercises or your experiences while doing them a part of the story, then your mind will ask: Why am I doing the exercises if I've already achieved levitation? You will have set up a contradiction in thought and defeat yourself before you even begin.

Concept four: You must create in your story a moment where you are thankful for the ability (levitation) that you have mastered. It should be thankfulness that you are still alive because of your mastered ability.

A famous philosopher once asked a question: If I can remember the past, why then can I not remember the future? In thought, there is no such thing as past or future; there is only a constantly moving now. So if you give thanks now for something that will not be achieved until later in the future and the future does not truly exist, can you really say you have not achieved it now? I know this may seem like a Zen riddle, but I'm teaching you an ancient secret to change your reality. As I asked earlier, have you ever been thankful for something you have not received?

Now comes another concept that I haven't mentioned to this point.

Concept five: Don't talk about what you are doing to anyone. Keep it a secret, and it will gain power in your life; talk about it, and you will only dissipate the energy of thought necessary for levitation to become a reality for you.

We all love to talk. Let's face it—we are creatures of communication. When people stop talking, even wars break out, so why would I ask you to fight the desire to talk about something you're trying to accomplish (in this case, levitation)? The answer is vacuum. In a universe of dissipated thoughts, one mind solely concentrated on an outcome not yet accomplished creates a vacuum of thought energy you would not believe. The universe abhors a vacuum and will do anything to fill it, so through silence, you will gain the attention of all that is. Know this also: You will be aided in your quest, and the vacuum will be filled.

This final concept is not a part of the story method I've outlined in the Foundation Technique, but it is not an afterthought either. Don't waste your work by dissipating all that effort through bragging or filling some misbegotten need to share. Even if you decide to work with another person on the goal of levitation, which is perfectly acceptable, avoid talking with each other about it. Believe me, you will get off the floor much faster.

The Nuts and Bolts of the Foundation Technique: Observation with Emotion

That wraps up the basic concepts, so now let's get down to the nuts and bolts making and how long to listen to the story you've created.

If you can walk down an alley or hallway, you can write about it. That's all story making really is—putting into words what you normally don't pay attention to all day. When you walk down a hall, for instance, ask yourself some questions: Is it carpeted? Is the carpet thick or thin? Is there padding under it? Does it seem to slow me down, or does it feel good under my feet? What colors are the walls? Are they rough or smooth? Are there any windows?

Now let's make a Foundation Technique story with the questions we've just asked ourselves.

As I walk down the hallway on my way to end the life of the miserable little man responsible for my family's death, I notice the worn, drab, reddish carpet that covers this hallway that feels like quicksand under my feet. It isn't the carpet itself but rather the thick padding under it that gives it this slowing effect. It reminds me of walking through mud on my way to hell. The walls must

have been painted by a manic-depressive: indecisive green with a rough texture to cover the unevenness of the surface. What a contrast to the carpet. It was like someone tried to cheer up a mental ward.

There are windows here and there that look down on a parking garage six stories below; across from that, a gray building without personality (much like the one I am in) catches my eye. I notice that even the light has a gray tint to it as it passes through these bleak portals. Even the air smells gray.

Let's stop there and see what I've done. I have taken my observations and painted a picture with words for your mind. I've added drama and a sense of dread because this fictitious killing about to take place is not a happy experience. This is the first part of a successful Foundation Technique story: Make observations and paint a word picture that your mind can live in. Try to notice the little things—they will put you more fully into the story—and use your emotional responses to describe them. Also remember that you have five senses, so use them all. This makes the story more personal, it helps you be there more fully, and it also adds a time element to the story.

The Plot or the Plan of Action

The second thing you need is a plot. "Plot" is just another word for a plan of action. You make a plan of action every day. When you go to the store, for instance, do you make a list of things you intend to buy? Do you mentally figure out which route you're going to take to actually get to the store? Once you're in the store, do you figure out a walking route to get the items on your list to save yourself extra steps?

All of these—the list, the route to the store, the walking route in the store—are plots or plans of action. Without plots, life would be unthinkably hard. Even a walk around the block would be impossible if you didn't pay attention to where you were going and have a plan of action for getting back to the place you started from. Again, it's about asking questions. This time you're not so much interested in the details around you as you are in the pathway to your goal and the stopping points, areas where you can go fast and places you must go slowly.

When you reach the desired point in your plan, what takes place? What goes wrong so that you must use your ability to levitate to save yourself? What happens after you save yourself? Think of your plan of action as having three distinctive points: a beginning, a middle, and an end. The mental picture painting I described a few paragraphs back is the glue that brings these three points together to form a successful Foundation Technique story. Above all, keep it simple and make it personal. This is your story.

The Length of Your Story

Your Foundation Technique story should be no longer than about ten or fifteen minutes because the intensity you are trying to achieve goes away after that. Let's face it. We are a hardworking race of people who just don't have a lot of time on our hands. In India, a practitioner of meditation might have hours to focus on his belly button, but he doesn't have a job or a family to feed either. I mean no insult to those who practice meditation; I'm just trying to point out that the time and energy commitment can be costly for such practices. The Foundation Technique is for people who feel like they could be a guru if life would just stop getting in the way.

As far as doing it in the morning or at night, I'll leave that to you. I generally do mine at night because I'm a night person, but that's me. You do it when you want to. Just make sure you won't be disturbed; silence the phones and close the doors. This is your time and no one else's.

Survival Levitation

The Final Pieces (and How to Cheat)

When I first formulated the Foundation Technique, I tried to use it as a pure meditation technique. I'd form the story on paper and then try to play it accurately in my mind. Much to my dismay, I found that I'd forget major parts of the story and sometimes drift so far from the plot that the story became a glorified daydream.

The best way I found to do the Foundation Technique was to record the story on a cassette recorder. Nowadays I notice digital recorders are replacing the cassette recorder, and some of these units have tremendous storage capacity for the money. Digital recorders are also a lot smaller and are much more mobile. Unlike the cassette recorder, a digital recorder allows you to place the stories in folders instead of relying on a tape position counter, and it's nice to have your stories in their own folders and still be able to record a shopping list in the main segment. Whichever method you use, you will find it's so much easier to record your stories and play them back as opposed to trying to use them as a style of meditation.

Earlier in this chapter, I told you to use your fear to your advantage, but you can also use someone else's story of fear. When the story puts the main character in a bad position where he or she is going to die and then at the last minute finds a way of escape, all you have to do is switch the author's solution with one that allows levitation to be the answer and replace the endangered character with yourself.

Many talented authors spend hours creating dangerous scenarios that would scare the pants off any sane human, so why not use them. Fantasy is good and will keep your sessions interesting. In different Foundation Technique stories, I've been a firefighter, an assassin, a Ninja, and an airline disaster victim.

The main difference between a Foundation Technique story and a story in a book is the markers, which are the things you experience as the story progresses—things like "I passed the third window on my right as I ran and noticed this one was cracked," or "My foot splashed down in a puddle on the road as I looked behind me." Because Foundation Technique stories are simpler than a story you might read in a book, you need to add markers to really put yourself in the story; markers also add time and a sense of drama to the story.

Unlike stories in a book with multiple timelines and several different characters, Foundation Technique stories are all about you and what is happening to you right now, so by placing markers in the story, you are literally counting your progress through the story.

It's a good idea to mix your stories up. I say this for two reasons: First, it just keeps things interesting; second, if you concentrate on one story too long, you will start noticing key aspects of your story appearing in your life. Concentrated thought felt with intense emotion will definitely start to shape your reality, so keep several stories available for the Foundation Technique. The inner mind always affects the outer world.

Remember when I told you that the mind already understands this and defends against this effect by keeping you scatterbrained (thoughts all over the place)? It's just a natural thing we do to try and stabilize our reality, so be smart and use multiple stories. Instead of being scatterbrained, be "scatter-storied." Also from a mental standpoint, you're telling yourself it's OK to use levitation in multiple scenarios and not just for one key event.

If you only exercise a muscle with a limited range of motion, it will only be strong in that limited range, and if you try to stress it further, you will usually find it's much weaker at a range past its normal workout range. The mind is no different.

A Final Story to Help You Understand the Importance of Giving Yourself Permission

In Africa and in Asia, there are several stories that have surfaced about apes that have taken human babies to rear as their own, but usually these babies die from exposure and the unintentional rough treatment of the apes that take them. Human infants are just not as tough as our ape counterparts in the wild. Every once in a while, however, one does survive and grows up believing he or she is an ape.

This happened with a group of orangutans that had stolen a human male child and raised it as their own. When the child was observed in the wild living with the group of orangutans, preparations were made to trap the child and take him back to civilization, where a group of doctors were ready to help. (This has happened more than once, but this child's story is slightly more interesting than the others that I have read.)

Once the child was brought to the doctors who had decided to treat him, efforts started immediately to acclimate the child to his human origins. The doctors noted severe scoliosis of his spine and damage to his hands and shoulders from moving around as orangutans move; his hips were also deformed, and his body in general was in bad shape from living as an ape. After treating his physical issues as best they could, the doctors next moved to teach the boy human customs and manners.

The first thing they did was to put clothes on the boy. The lad took the clothing off almost immediately, so the doctors put the clothing back on him. The second time the boy was dressed in human clothes, he did not remove them but instead chose to keep the clothing on. The doctors saw this as a sign of success—until they did the exact same thing to an orangutan. As was the case with the boy, the orangutan took the clothing off the first time it was dressed but the second time kept the clothing on.

The same thing happened with using eating utensils and learning to sit at a table. Each time the doctors thought they had achieved success with the boy, they found that an orangutan would do exactly the same thing the boy was doing. What's more, the learning curve was the same even though it should have been faster for a human to pick up the new behavioral patterns.

This is one of those stories that does not end well. Despite all the months of work that went into reconditioning this boy by some of the top psychologists of the day, a couple of years later the boy (by then a teenager) died in captivity, still believing he was an orangutan. In fact, the few stories that I've managed to dig up on humans being raised by animals seem to end the same way: They just don't seem to be able to acclimate to their human origins. That is sad indeed.

I'm not going to be as brave and bold as to say that I'm smarter than the trained doctors who tried to treat this boy, but I will say this: They did not ask the right questions. Although the answer was right in front of their faces, they did not see it. In the doctors' defense, understanding what they missed would not have brought the boy back to being human, but it would have helped them realize just how deep the hole really was and why they failed so completely. Are you curious about what it was they missed?

It goes a little something like this. Psychologists are quick to point out that humans have no instincts and that everything a human is and does has to be learned. I guarantee that the boy in question was never dressed in human clothing while he was living in the wild with his orangutan group, nor did he ever learn about eating utensils or any of the other things that the doctors tried to recondition him with. Despite having no knowledge of how an orangutan would act when exposed to these new things and behaviors, he did exactly what an orangutan would do. Just because he was raised as an orangutan does not take away from the fact that the boy was human, so it begs the question of how the boy pulled these orangutan behaviors out of thin air.

Survival Levitation

If you see things from my viewpoint, it's easy to understand that the thought that defined the orangutans was also the thought that defined the boy. Once that deep-seated thought matrix was accepted, the boy had no option but to act as an orangutan acts. Even the parts of orangutan behavior he had never learned would be accessible to him because the thought matrix has predefined rules built right into it. These thought constructs exist all around us, and we never really see them because thought is so closely tied to what it defines that the object and the thought behind it are seamless—one can't exist without the other.

I'm going to share a secret with you even though it is an advanced magical truth (and a higher Magus might frown on me for revealing it) because understanding it will help you to really tie together what I'm telling you. In times not too far removed from the present, it was taught to Shaman and Magus alike that if you knew the true name of something, you could control and change it in any way that you needed to as long as you didn't create a paradox within the overall matrix of reality itself.

Hollywood jumped on this theme. In a couple of movies I've seen, a wizard speaks the true name of a dragon or an old tree or something else he or she wishes to control; suddenly the animal or the object obeys the whim of the wizard without question. Usually the names are exotic sounding and mysterious to add drama to the movie, but this is a bunch of nonsense and totally misses the mark.

Are you ready for the truth? When a Shaman and a Magus refer to knowing the true name of something, they are talking about getting into the thought essence that makes and defines the object or entity they wish to control. How this is done is something I cannot share with you because it is indeed a dangerous secret that can really screw things up (and survival levitation is not really about this anyway), but I do want you to understand it's there.

It is said that in times of old one of the tests of a high druid was to reverse the course of a river with his mind alone. At face value, you might think he would have to have tremendous telekinetic ability to do such a feat, but that is not how it was done. It was done by the druid becoming a part of the thought that made and defined the river and convincing it that it was going in the wrong direction. The river would then change its own direction. It sounds simple, but it was something a high druid had to train his whole life to achieve. That is the power of knowing something's true name.

When we think of the boy who accepted the thought matrix of an orangutan as his own and, more importantly, was accepted by the orangutan thought matrix as one of its own, we can start to see why the doctors failed so completely in their attempts at reconditioning the child in this trap of thought to be human again. It can't be done from the outside with clothing, eating utensils, or any of the behavior modification methods modern psychology can dream up.

It would have to be done from the standpoint of removing the old orangutan thought matrix and replacing it with the one that defines humans. In the process, you would have to rip apart the boy's psyche, which would probably kill him, but those pesky orangutan behavioral patterns would be gone.

When you started to read how the Foundation Technique works, you might have asked yourself why my method is so dark, why I ask you to face your own death and use strong fear to further your progression, why I ask you to invoke such strong emotion. I'm teaching you to know your own true name, to get inside your own true thought construct and change it. It's not as easy as a hypnotist or some New Age "fluff bunny" might have you believe. It takes work to get your thought matrix's attention.

As we learned from the failure of the intelligent doctors who worked with the boy who lived with the orangutans, changing a thought is no easy thing. This is why I give you the Foundation Techn. why it is the way it is. Quite frankly, changing a thought th and defines something or someone is a profound undertakin, underestimate the effort involved in such an undertaking.

There is one final thing I must teach you about the Foundation Technique: It is not a stand-alone exercise. You must bring whatever you are trying to achieve with it into the physical realm. In the case of levitation, you will be learning the physical exercises shortly, but if you want to use it for something else, remember to devise a way to practice this wanted ability in real time and in a real environment.

AN EXERCISE TO BUILD INTERNAL ENERGY

(The Breath of the Magus)

Let's face it, as we get older, we lose vitality and our energy seems to diminish. If you're young, you can probably skip this section completely. If you're older and would like to achieve levitation, it may help to spend a little time each day with this exercise.

At one time, I studied Pranayama, which is a breathing exercise that the folks in India claim they invented. The practice entails breathing in slowly, holding the breath for a set amount of time, and releasing it slowly. The cycle itself is one to four to two seconds: For every one second you take a breath, you hold it for four seconds and release it for two seconds. The beginning cycle is four seconds of breathing in, sixteen seconds of holding the breath, and eight seconds of releasing the breath.

The times go up from there. This may sound easy, but after you do it awhile, you realize it's much harder than it first appears. Thank God for spiritual advisers. My spiritual adviser rarely speaks, but when she does, it's usually interesting. As I struggled with Pranayama, she cut in and told me I was doing it wrong. Like so many of our communications, it was followed by a burst of understanding on the proper way of doing it.

To do the breath of the Magus, all you have to do is breathe in slowly and then—instead of holding the breath—just arrest the breath without clamping down. You should be able to draw in more air without releasing anything in your throat or chest. It helps if you don't fill your lungs full of air but rather stop about halfway; there is little discomfort with this method. Now with the breath stopped, I want you to feel like you're still drawing in air without actually doing it. You know what it feels like to take air into your lungs, so instead of doing it, just start to do it and hold the sensation of inhaling. Remember that your lungs are about half full of air, so it's like you're still breathing in without more air filling your lungs.

Hold the inhaling sensation for as long as is comfortable; then slowly release the breath. Something else that helps me is to mentally hear the sound of the inhaling of breath in my mind. Listen to yourself breathe in a few times and then create that sound in your imagination without actually breathing in. It's like visualization with your ears instead of your eyes.

What you're actually doing is using the inhaling of breath as a means to pull energy into the body. The inhaling of breath is nature's little vacuum. The feeling of inhaling without pulling in air still creates a vacuum; the only difference is that the body pulls in raw life force instead of air. The universe detests a vacuum and will supply matter or energy to fill it.

You don't have to do this exercise for extended periods of time. It is a very powerful method for bringing in life force, so doing it for five to ten minutes a session is fine. I've done it longer, but then I would notice that everything metallic started zapping me. At one point I had to start putting on leather gloves just to get into my car (it's disconcerting to reach for your car door handle and have a two-inch blue spark nail you). If you start having painful electrical problems like this, cut back on your session times. Too much static electricity in your body can make you afraid to touch anything—not to mention the really bad looks you get when you pet your cat.

You can do this exercise while standing or sitting. If you choose to do it while standing, please hold onto something to help balance yourself. I also have to tell you that this exercise feels really funny at first, so please give yourself time to get used to it. If you go slowly, you will find this exercise works really well, but if you try to force it, you'll just end up panting like a hot puppy.

What do I mean by forcing it? There are two ways people generally force this exercise: They arrest the breath too long, or they fill their lungs way too full of air. If you feel uncomfortable at all doing this exercise, you're doing it wrong. Relax and let the energy flow into you like a soft, gentle cloud; if you're tense and uncomfortable, there can be no energy flow.

Don't worry about counting the seconds of breathing in, holding the breath, and breathing out the air. The important part is the arresting of the breath with the feeling of inhaling without taking in more air. On the inhaling, go slowly; on the exhaling, go even more slowly. You may wonder why I say to go slowly. It's actually quite simple really. When you first eat a meal, does it become a part of you right away? If it did, I can guarantee there would be no fat people. Think of taking a bite of donut and seeing an immediate reaction in your thighs—we'd throw the evil thing away right then! Due to the process of assimilation, that donut is going to take hours to make it to your thighs, so the bakery business is safe today because of this delay.

The energy you are pulling in has not had a chance to become part of your body either. The energy is raw and requires time to align itself with your individual vibratory rate. This happens faster than the digestion of food, but it still takes time. This is why we breathe in slowly and exhale even more slowly. If you breathe in quickly, you disturb the energy you've already pulled into yourself; if you breathe out quickly, you literally push the energy right out of yourself with the breath. The way to think about the energy you are pulling in is that it's like a fragile wisp of light or a cloud that must be treated gently or else you'll lose it.

Finally, let's look at the fact that sometimes you just have to breathe normally for a few seconds when doing this exercise. It happens to me all the time. I'll be going along with the exercise just fine, and suddenly my body just has to take a few normal breaths. When this happens, you must breathe slowly; avoid the desire to pant. In a few seconds, your desire to pant will normalize, and then you can return to the exercise.

It doesn't hurt a thing to take normal breaths during the exercise. In time, you will be able to stick with the exercise longer as you gain control over your breathing. The only way you can fail is if you allow yourself to jerk the breath in and out quickly because this will force the energy you have gathered out of your body before it has a chance to become part of you.

When I do this exercise, I get the impression that lines of energy are coming into me from all sides. These lines look like spider webs: They are clear, they look wet, and they glisten. When I do this exercise outside, I notice a feeling of moisture on my skin, and this is one of the things I look for as a sign that I'm doing the breath of the Magus properly.

Sweating and shaking sometimes happen with this exercise. If this bothers you, discontinue this practice immediately. I've personally felt the shaking, but I know that it's just a sign of progress. The same is true of the sweating. With the sweating, rub yourself down after the session because your body is getting rid of poisons. The rubdown breaks up blockages under the skin of both energy and poisons.

There is one thing that all the animals and plants on this planet do to take in energy: They *inhale*. What I've just shown you is how to use the inhaling as a means of pulling in tremendous energy. The inhaling is what makes life happen, and the exhaling is the last thing we do before we die.

This is all there is to the breath of the Magus, but don't let its simple nature fool you. It's a very powerful exercise. That said, let's continue.

UNDERSTANDING THE MOVEMENT OF ENERGY

Are you ready for a little secret? You already know how to levitate—in fact you've been doing it all your life. I don't mean you've actually left the ground and risen into the air, but you have been moving around the energy necessary for levitation to happen ever since you learned to crawl. Have you ever noticed how hard it is to pick up an animal that does not wish to be handled? The same is true of a baby. When he or she wishes to be picked up, it's fairly easy to do so, but when the baby doesn't want to be picked up, you hear parents say things like "My goodness, you're getting heavy" or "You feel like you weigh a ton."

Animals or babies who do not wish to be picked up will automatically push the energy in their bodies down; if you watch them, you will see that they are looking down at the ground. On the other hand, if they want to be picked up, you will notice that they are lighter and more relaxed, and if you look at them, you will notice that they are looking up. Even without being taught, they know that their intent directs the flow of their energy.

What do I mean by intent directing the flow of energy? Let's say you intend to move forward. The energy inside your body will then shift forward in the direction of your intent. If you attempt to move an object that weighs as much as you do, you will notice that it is much harder to move (people often call this the difference between moving live weight and moving dead weight). The only real difference is that in dead weight, the energy inside the object does not move.

You are a creature of energy as well as matter. Are you curious how much matter is really involved in your body? Scientists have calculated that if you removed all the space in the body—all the space that exists between the organs, cells, and even the atoms themselves—you could fit three people on the head of a pin and they would have enough room to dance if they wanted to. What does the rest of the body consist of? As I said earlier, the rest of your body is energy and a whole lot of space.

I'm going to go out on a limb and say something from my personal experience as a person who understands levitation: Gravity does not affect matter; it only affects energy. Because matter and energy are so closely tied together, it appears that matter is being affected by gravity, but I just don't believe it to be true. I believe our present understanding of physics, matter, and energy is basically flawed. We don't see that a large part of the energy that is localized within matter is simply floating around in the tremendous spaces between the particles and that its only real connection with matter is its vibratory rate.

In this regard, I believe energy stabilizes matter so that it can exist as we know it. I'd like you to do a little experiment for me. It's time to prove to you that the energy inside your body does move to help you move. If you have just eaten a meal, please wait a couple of hours before trying the preparation exercises or any of the actual exercises below (a full tummy makes it hard to feel the energy inside your body). Remember, though, that you don't want to be hungry either.

Preparation Exercise One

Stand in a normal manner with your hands down at your sides. Relax and think "I'm going to take a step forward." Please understand there's a difference between thinking you're going to step forward and intending to do so. I want you to really intend to step forward. Now I want you to really feel what's going on inside your body as you take a step forward. Good. Now we're going to do the same thing backward. Think "I'm going to step backward." Again be mindful of the intent to take a step backward, and really feel what's happening here.

If you really stop and concentrate and *feel,* you will notice that before you move and sometimes even when you think about moving, there's a shift inside you. It has nothing to do with your balance or your muscles, although we mistake it for balance. This is much more subtle; this is your energy moving in the direction of your intended motion.

Preparation Exercise Two

OK, let's take it one step further. Now I'm going to show you how powerful that subtle energy shift really is. I want you to think "I'm going to take a step forward." Get your body ready to take a step forward in every way—I mean really *feel* like you're going to step forward. It's the *feeling* that is so important here. Do you have yourself really primed for that step forward? Good.

Instead, I want you to step backward. That's right; I want you to go in the opposite direction from the way you intended to go. If you really were believing that you were going to step forward and then stepped back instead, you will notice that it really felt funny. Most of the people I have do this simple demonstration say it felt as if something was pulling them in the direction that they had intended to travel, and some can't actually even go in the opposite direction.

Now I want you to get yourself ready to step backward. Really believe you're going to take a step backward. Now take a step forward, again going in the opposite direction from the way you intended to go. Are you starting to feel what I'm talking about? It is kind of a bizarre feeling to go against your intended direction, isn't it?

You might have noticed that I called these preparation exercises and not just experiments. If you do the actual exercise I've given below every day for a couple of weeks, you will start to notice that you can shift your energy around without having to fool yourself anymore; you won't have to intend forward motion just to make your energy move forward. You will start to move your energy with your will alone, and that's how we start down the road to levitation.

Different people feel it in different ways. Some folks say they can feel the shift of energy from front to back; some people I've had do this say it's like pressure in the direction they intend to travel; a few folks tell me it feels like heat on the side of their intended direction; and with some, they tell me it's like they just become more aware of their body on the side facing the direction of intended travel.

With me, it feels like a shift inside and then more of a building in the body toward the direction of my intent. I will start to lose my balance in the direction of my intended travel; at that point, I shift my energy in the opposite direction and can usually catch it without taking a step.

However it feels to you is right for you. What I'm trying to get you to feel is how your body feels when your energy moves when you intend to go in a certain direction. Then I want you to get to the point where you can get that feeling without intending to move—that's right, just moving the energy inside.

Vectoring Exercise

This teaching is actually twofold: One, I'm teaching you to learn to move the energy in your body; two, I'm teaching you to vector your energy. What does "vector your energy" mean? Rather than go into the complexities of vectors and resultant energy forces, let me explain it this way. When you levitate the first couple of times, you probably won't go straight up; you usually slide across the ground until you crash into something.

Most folks will believe they just lost their balance because that's what it feels like. Why does this happen? The short answer is that your energy is not going evenly in an upward direction and that you usually don't have enough force. You lack stability; like a piece of cardboard in a windstorm, you go all over the place.

So when I say "vector your energy," I mean that you have to push your energy up to levitate and push it in the opposite direction from which you will find yourself sliding. Your main energy flow is up, with a lean in it so to speak, so you can stay in one spot. If you are one of the lucky ones who naturally stay in one spot, with a slight vectoring of your energy you will find you can move while levitating.

OK, let's learn to do it. Tie two pieces of line, rope, or whatever between two solid anchor points in your house. Make it so that when you hold these lines in either hand, your hands are slightly away from the sides of your body and your arms are hanging down in a relaxed manner. What you don't want to do is crucify yourself—you don't want your arms straight out from your sides. The reason we hold onto these two lines is safety; when you feel safe, you can fully concentrate on the energy inside.

After making sure you won't fall, put your feet together and relax. Remember—you can't use your muscles. You must relax your body, especially your ankles and feet because these are your pivot points. Get it in your mind that you're just about to take a step forward and wait for the feeling of your balance shifting, but don't lean into it or fight against it. It's this subtle feeling of shift that we're after. If you're totally relaxed and not using your muscles, this isn't a balance shift at all but rather an energy shift.

At first, this feeling will be weak and your body will just stay standing straight up, but after working with this exercise for a while, you will notice a definite movement of energy in your body; also your body will start to move forward as you gain proficiency with this exercise. Since your feet are together and not moving, you may have to take a step forward to steady yourself, which is the reason for the ropes. No falling allowed!

I have to warn you that it's real easy to cheat with this exercise and start using your muscles to move yourself around. If you catch yourself starting to use your muscles, remind yourself to relax and again just use that feeling of energy shifting inside your body. Remember—it's the feeling of taking a step forward.

As you lean forward, try to get the feeling of taking a step backward, which will shift your energy to the rear of your body. If you are not leaning too far forward, you will be able to catch yourself and your body will once again stand straight up. When you first begin to have success with vectoring your energy, remember to catch it while your body's lean is small. This will save time stumbling around holding onto your safety ropes for dear life.

As I put this exercise down on paper, I know this is possibly one of the most frustrating parts of learning levitation. When you first start, you may feel like I'm crazy for having you do something you can hardly feel. Your body won't move much or move at all at first. If you stick with it, though, you will find that you will be able to feel the energy shift inside your body more and much faster. You will also find your body will lean farther and faster, and sometimes it will be like you're suddenly falling forward.

If you start to fall, you can always take a step forward and that will stop it, as I stated earlier. Don't forget the ropes are also there for balance, but as time goes on, you will find yourself using safety measures less and less often. I have found myself what I thought was way too far into a lean, only to push the energy in the opposite direction and recover without having to catch myself with a step or use my ropes. You will also get there.

As I stated earlier, it is easy to cheat with the vectoring exercise and use your muscles to move yourself around, but I have to warn you that it's also easy to do the opposite. When you move your energy forward, your body will tend to move with it. Because you have been doing this all your life, you might feel like your body's moving because you have engaged your muscles, but if you are totally relaxed, this isn't true.

When I first started using the vectoring exercise, I felt as if it must be my muscles moving me around because how else could my body start to lean just because I felt my energy move forward? Remember—matter and energy are tied so closely together that they sometimes feel like the same thing. That's why this exercise can be so frustrating; you constantly have to monitor yourself not to aid it by using your muscles and not to fight against it by thinking you're using your muscles.

When you move your energy, your body will move. It feels like you're shifting your balance, and you are, but you're not using your muscles to do it. This is a sign of success with this exercise. Don't disbelieve your incredible success just because vectoring feels like something totally natural. It is totally natural for you to move your energy before you actually move your body, and it's also natural for your body to move with your energy, although this may be surprising at first. I'm just teaching you how to consciously take control of this incredible body-moving force.

I have just described how to vector your energy to the front of your body and catch it with a rear energy reversal. It's a little scarier to do it to the rear and then catch it with a front energy reversal, but that's why we have the safety ropes. Again, relax your body, especially your ankles and feet. Get that feeling of taking a step backward, and wait for your energy to respond and your body to lean backward. Don't go too far before reversing your energy to the front because this is a much more disconcerting feeling.

Vectoring will save your life if you ever find yourself teetering on the brink of a large cliff. Unlike the poor guy who finds himself on the edge of a cliff, arms windmilling and hoping to God he will regain his balance, you will be able to reverse your energy and take a step back; then you can grab the guy who's windmilling his arms before he falls to his death. You can even use it to walk on a window ledge if you just vector your energy toward the building. The ability to vector will really help your balance and confidence, so it's kind of a nice thing to know how to do.

EXERCISES TO BUILD YOUR ABILITY TO LEVITATE

By learning to vector, you're knocking at the door of levitation. Vectoring is how we start to learn to move energy, but by itself it's not enough. We have to have a way of forcing ourselves to learn to push our energy up when we are standing up, which is hard to feel because it's just not something we normally do. That said, most of you have already felt the feeling of partial levitation at least once in your life.

Let me tell you how it happened. Usually it takes place on a steep staircase or on a hill that you're about to go down. Most psychologists call this vertigo due to situational acrophobia. Translated, it means you're disoriented and maybe even dizzy because you're afraid of falling down the staircase or the hill.

Have you ever noticed that if someone is going to fall down a staircase, the fall will usually begin at the top of the stairs and not at the middle or the bottom of the stairs? It sounds like a Murphy's law kind of thing but really isn't. It would be better to fall from the middle or the bottom of the stairs, wouldn't it? Your chances of getting hurt would be greatly reduced! Sadly this just isn't the way it usually works out.

Let me tell you why. If you watch some people standing at the top of a tall staircase or a steep hill, you will sometimes notice that they are leaning slightly backward, that their neck is extended, and that they're looking down their nose at the impending doom they're about to experience. While not being aware of it, these people have already vectored their energy up and to the rear of their body—they are already in a state of partial levitation without even realizing it.

As they take the first step down, they don't have their total weight on that foot because their energy has been pulled up in their body. (This is why if you're going to slip, this is when it will happen.) Less weight equals less friction, which equals less stability. This is why those first couple of steps on that high staircase or steep hill feel kind of bouncy. Also with their energy vectored to the rear of their body, their feet will tend to slip out from under them to the front. That's a lot of bad stuff to deal with on the first couple of steps; believe me, the odds are against them for making it to the bottom unscathed.

The reason I'm telling you all this is twofold: One, I want you to remember how it felt to push your energy up in your body if you have ever experienced vertigo; two, I want you to do the opposite if you ever face the high staircase or steep hill situation. I want you to push your energy down. In the martial arts, this technique is called "rooting."

I have had the honor of seeing an aikido master root himself and have twelve students try to push him off the spot he stood on; they could not do it. A U.S. Special Forces captain who held a black belt in judo also did a similar demonstration by playing tug-of-war with an entire squad of strong young men when I was in the military. Once he rooted, they could not budge him either. Even though it may feel wrong, remember—when going down, push your energy down!

Learning to Move the Energy
Up and Making It Strong

In this section, I'm going to show you a very simple exercise that will start you down the path to actual levitation. In order to learn levitation, I have to get you in touch with the feeling of moving your energy up, and to do this, I'm going to ask you to do something that may sound a little crazy: You need to weight yourself down. When I say this, I know you're probably a little confused, but let me explain.

In certain martial arts, they do a funny little exercise where they stand and put their forearms under a bar. By pushing up with the palms up and fingers extended, the martial artist creates a barrier to the natural energy flow through the hands. The martial artist then pushes the energy out of the hands with the will of his or her mind; the bar across the forearms just makes it so the person doing the exercise can feel the energy extending through his or her hands (it's the same concept as pinching off a hose at the end to make the water flow stronger).

After learning to extend energy through and out of the hands this way, the martial artist can hit with a lot more impact. Bruce Lee used to do this exercise quite religiously. Believe me when I say this: That little guy could swat! Bruce Lee also publicly denounced what he considered foolish mystical activities found in many forms of the martial arts, so there had to be something to the movement of energy or he would not have even messed with it.

When I say to weight yourself down, I do not mean a lot of weight. Create some sandbags that weigh no more than ten pounds, and make them long and slender so they drape over your body. As you put the bags together, remember to put the sand in plastic bags first before you put it in the cloth part of the bags, or you will have sand all over your house (I learned this the hard way).

If you are older or have an injured back or neck, you don't have to make the sandbags ten pounds; make them a weight that is comfortable for you and that won't cause injury. The weight is not nearly as important as the feeling of something pressing down on you.

To do this exercise in the sitting position, drape a sandbag over each shoulder, over each thigh, and over your head; also place a weight in each hand, and have your hands dangle down by your sides unsupported. Again, this is not really about the weight as much as it's about the feeling of something pressing you down, so don't injure yourself. It takes just an instant to hurt yourself and sometimes a lifetime to heal (if you heal at all). Safety first!

Now that you're all comfy, let's start the exercise. We are going to play a little pretend game and make-believe that we have a lot more weight on ourselves than we actually do. The weights you are using are just draped over your shoulders, thighs, and head, but in our game we are going to pretend that they're tied on and we can't shake them. Also I want you to get the feeling that you're at the bottom of a pool under nine feet of water. Don't worry about visualizing this scene as if you are there because that's not important; the game only adds drama and a little sense of desperation to the exercise.

Whatever you do, don't stop breathing as if you're really under water because it is not necessary and will mess with your natural energy flow. What you want is the feeling of being tied down at the bottom of a pool and trying desperately to get to the surface.

Phase one

Dynamic tension is a style of strength training where you push against an imaginary weight. Sometimes people who do this style of exercise will add a small amount of weight to make it more real. Unlike dynamic tension, we don't want to do a full range of motion with the weights we are using; also keep in mind that we don't want to strain because we are not trying to build muscle. We are learning to direct energy, so push up against the weights on your shoulders, thighs, and head with intensity, but don't strain. The feeling here is, "If I could just push through these weights, I could get to the surface of the pool."

Pay close attention to the weights on your shoulders, thighs, and head as you look up at the ceiling and pretend that the ceiling is the top of the pool you're weighted down in. Look with your eyes and don't lean your head back because this will put an unfamiliar strain on your neck. Remember—intent directs energy flow. If you're thinking about the bags on your shoulders, thighs, and head and are looking at the ceiling, the ceiling is where your energy will go. You want to push up for about ten seconds and then relax.

Phase two

Now with this feeling that you are trapped and weighted down at the bottom of a pool and the ceiling is the surface of the water, try to get the same feeling of push as you did in phase one without using your muscles. Think "Up, up, up. I'm going to float up." Push your energy right through the weights that are holding you down. Try to remember what it felt like to float to the surface of a pool for that breath of air your body so desperately needed.

It's just like learning to vector your energy forward. Remember how I told you to get the feeling of "I'm going to step forward"? This time we are moving the energy up through the weights, and the feeling is "I'm going to float to the surface of this pool after I get through the weights that are holding me down."

Remember to pay close attention to the weights on your shoulders, thighs, and head and to push the energy through the weights with the same intensity as you did when you were pushing with your muscles, but you must remain relaxed. Remember to look at the ceiling. Throughout this phase, you must remain relaxed and only push with your energy. Keep breathing and push harder on the exhaling, as this is when your body naturally extends energy. Do this phase for about twenty or thirty seconds.

The reason we use the weights, besides the fact that they help you feel your energy, is that we mentally mimic the feeling of pushing through them as we did when we were actually lifting them. The weights will help you get in touch with your energy much faster because pushing your energy up through a barrier helps you really feel the movement of energy in your body.

Levitation is all about the movement of energy in your body, and what I'm teaching you is the fast track to this ability. If this seems strange or frustrating at first, stick with it and you will be amazed at how much easier it will be to move the energy in your body after doing these simple exercises.

After the twenty or thirty seconds of phase two have passed, I want you to again push up against the weights with your muscles as I had you do in phase one for about ten seconds. Then relax and repeat phase two of this exercise for twenty or thirty seconds. Continue alternating between phase one and phase two for about ten or fifteen minutes.

Just like the amount of weight, the time is not set in stone, so if you start to feel tired and want to quit after five or seven minutes, do so. I can't know your age or fitness level, and the last thing I want you to do is hurt yourself. It's only common sense that learning new survival abilities should not threaten your survival, so do what you can do and be proud of it.

Phase three

For this final phase, you simply take the weights off your body and then stand up and take hold of the ropes you used for vectoring, making sure you have some slack in each rope. You don't want a lot of slack so that if you do suddenly need to stabilize your balance, you can, but you do need a little so you are standing free. Now push the energy in your body up as you did when the weights were on you.

Again look up and make-believe that the ceiling is the top of the water you need to get to so that you can take the breath you need to survive. Remember what it felt like to float up to the surface of water; really try to get that feeling, pushing your energy up as you do so. Make this phase last for a couple of minutes or as long as you want. I have to warn you that this is usually the time you will have your first levitation experience and that it may not be what you expect.

The first time you levitate, it will probably feel like you slipped or lost your balance. This is a great sign of progress, but it also makes it necessary to use the ropes to keep from falling. The reason for this is your body's own mechanics: Your muscles are holding you straight in the standing position, and to do this, there is all kinds of tension in your muscles, ligaments, and joints you're not even aware of.

A large part of your balance (or what you perceive to be your balance) is your connection with the floor. An example of what I'm talking about can be seen when people try to stand on wet ice: Their legs want to go all over the place, and they usually have to use a completely unfamiliar set of leg muscles to keep from falling. Whether you're standing on a completely friction-free surface like wet ice or you're levitating, the result is the same—your connection with the ground goes away, and you will tend to lose your balance.

You may have to go through this for quite a while before you actually get off the ground, but if you keep at it, you will get past this point. It helps to spend a little more time with the breath of the Magus exercise to ramp up your internal energy at this point.

Now that you have learned to do the weighted exercise in the seated position, you can also do it lying down. Everything is the same, but you don't push the energy up through your shoulders and head; instead, you push the energy forward (the feeling of "I'm going to take a step forward") if you're lying on your back or backward (the feeling of "I'm going to take a step backward") if you're lying on your stomach.

The end result is the same: You're pushing your energy up toward the ceiling. To get past the strangeness of the feeling of stepping forward or backward while lying down, I just pretend I'm standing up and pressed up against a wall. The nice thing about doing it lying down is that you can use more weights and put them on more parts of your body. It's that feeling of being held down and pushing your energy through the weights that is so important. I must caution you, though, to not get carried away and hurt yourself.

Phase three is also different. Get the weights off your body as before, but don't stand up. Push the energy forward as you did before if you're on your back, but the fact that you're already lying down means you don't need the safety ropes. Relax and remember to look up at the ceiling as you did before—intent directs energy flow. Concentrate solely on your energy moving forward in the body and don't worry about levitating. It will happen when you're ready.

As before, you will tend to slip before you can actually rise off the ground in a controlled manner. Again, this is a great sign of progress. (It may take some time to get past this point in development for some people.) Be patient, keep at it, and you will get there.

When most people think of levitation, they tend to think in terms of levitating while in the standing position. You might ask: Why would I ever need to learn to levitate lying down? Let's say you found yourself in a burning building and had to go through a ventilation shaft to reach safety. The only problem was that every time you touched the steel floor of this ventilation shaft, it burned you badly because of the fire raging outside. If you take the time to learn levitation while on your stomach and back and then find yourself in this situation, you would only have to vector your energy through your shoulders and head while levitating horizontally or use your hands only sparingly to navigate this hot box nightmare.

Let me give you another reason to learn this ability. You can move along the ground very quietly and quickly while exposing only a bare minimum of your body; just use your hands and toes to propel you and guide your direction. A soldier knows that crawling through brush or over land makes a lot of noise, which is why they are trained to crawl slowly.

A sniper knows that crawling through a field of tall grass will leave a very visible trail to any sentry in an elevated position, so snipers are trained to use their feet to push the grass back up behind them as they crawl. Neither method is perfect, so there will always be some noise or a visible trail left behind. If you learn horizontal levitation, both the noise and the trail are eliminated, and in the times that lie ahead for us, this may not be a bad skill to have.

Finally, the more ways you learn to move your energy, the faster your first true off-the-ground levitation experience will occur. Many times people can feel the energy moving better when they are lying down than when they are standing up, but perhaps with you it's the opposite. The simple fact is the more directions you can move internal energy, the stronger you're going to get at moving it. You can liken it to a body builder: If he only works on his arms, he's going to have really strong arms, but the rest of his body will be weak; if he works on his whole body, he will be much stronger overall.

The lying down version of the weighted exercise can also be of help to those of you who have trouble with vectoring. A few people I've tried to train have a real hard time with vectoring until they work with the floor style of this exercise. Even though doing the weighted exercises is traditionally something that's done after you get the concept of vectoring, sometimes it helps to do them first to loosen up the energy so you can really feel it during the vectoring exercises.

So there you have it. The vectoring will get you in touch with your energy, and the weighted exercises will make the movement of internal energy much stronger. If you think this is too simple, I'll tell you that many times it's the simple things in life that actually work. This system is simple and very effective. I used it while in the Navy to achieve my first levitation; my methods were a lot cruder, but the result was the same.

Let me tell you about it. I had been doing vectoring and the weighted exercises in one of the troop spaces that normally went unused on the troop transport ship I was assigned to. At that time, all this was just a theory I had stuck in my head and I had no idea if it would actually work. I had been doing the exercises for about a month and a half when I could get away from my normal duties, and I got pretty good at moving my internal energy up, forward, back, and down in my body. One day I was walking in a part of Sandi Ago that I had not been in before because (as usual) I was lost. There were warehouses all around me and no windows to be seen, so I started pushing the energy up as I walked.

I felt the lightness that usually came to me as I pushed the energy up while walking, but other than that I couldn't seem to get off the ground so to speak. So I continued pushing the energy up for about a block or so. I went to step off a really high curb to cross the street when it happened—I sailed right off the curb and did not touch the street I had been thinking I'd step down on; instead, I just kept going in the air for about four feet or so. I was young and had a habit of walking fast, especially when I was lost, so I had quite a lot of momentum to aid this unexpected flight; needless to say, I managed to scare myself silly.

I also noticed something about the movement of energy that kind of surprised me. After pushing up internal energy for a while as I did when I was walking, I found that just because I stopped focusing on the energy as I floated along, it didn't come down by itself, and I had to push the energy down to get back down to the street, so that's something you should keep in mind.

Make rooting or pushing the energy down part of your practice session. Trust me when I say this: Peddling your feet in the air in a panic while levitating will not get you back down to the ground. I know this from personal experience. But enough about me; let's get back to your development.

THE LEARNED ABILITY OF CONCENTRATION

Have you ever noticed that books dealing with the psychic sciences always tell you to visualize this or concentrate on that without ever teaching you how to visualize or concentrate? Have you noticed in this book that I have avoided using the word "visualize"? I get a real bang out of the books that tell you to visualize something as if you're actually there.

What they don't tell you is that it may take many years to develop the ability to visualize something with such single-minded concentration that you feel as if you're actually part of what you're visualizing. The inexperienced writers just throw it out there like it's the easiest thing in the world; no problem—you too can visualize like a yoga master in five easy lessons. Well, folks, I'm here to tell you it just doesn't work that way. Thank God visualization isn't necessary for the achievement of levitation. With levitation, it's all about feeling. I can't say the same thing is true of concentration. Almost all of us need a little help in this regard, so let me teach you how to concentrate like a Zen master.

Most people think they can concentrate but really don't know what true concentration is. True concentration is the total quieting of the talk, talk, talk that your brain does all day long; it is the quiet mind that makes it possible to do whatever you will as if it is the only thing in existence. The quiet mind allows the observer to come forth and fix into being whatever he or she chooses to observe. In quantum physics, they say that matter exists in all possible states at once until it is observed, but they will also tell you they don't know who or what the observer actually is. They can't see the forest for the trees because their minds are filled with too much chatter, and they have not learned the meditation of the final death.

The final death meditation was taught to me by a Zen Sufi who knew that I needed to learn to concentrate, and I'm very glad I learned it from him. There is no visualization in this form of Zazen (the term "Zazen" translates into "simply sitting" or "seated concentration" if you're curious). The reason it's called the final death meditation is because the last thing you do when you die is breathe out. My teacher told me that if you are awake and aware when you release this final breath, it will be the most intense exhaling of your entire life. The reference to your final breath is how you actually do this meditation—each breath is concentrated on as if it is your last.

The first phase of this meditation lasts for at least a month (and hopefully two or three months if you are so inclined). You don't want to rush to the next phase because it really is not a matter of graduation from one level to the next; it's about whether you're ready for the next phase. Each phase is only a refinement of the meditation, so if you don't feel like going any further, that's fine. It's all the same meditation.

To do the first phase and the following phases, first you look at something that is dark in color, like a brown door or a dark wall. (The surface should not have a lot of pattern, as this will become a distraction to your meditation.) Lower the lights, but don't do this meditation in the dark. Your eyes are kept open for this style of Zazen.

Inhale normally and slowly exhale, counting number one in your mind as you do so. The one is sounded in your mind all the time the breath is being exhaled, but don't say the number out loud. Then inhale normally and exhale slowly again, counting the number two.

The two is mentally sounded all the time the breath is being exhaled; don't repeat the number over and over again during the exhaling but rather think something like "Oooonnnneeee. Twwwwwooooo." Then take in another breath and exhale, counting mentally the number three ("Threeeeeeeeee"). Do this until you reach the number ten, and then start at number one again.

Do this for ten or fifteen minutes. Later on, as your ability to concentrate develops, you might want to do it longer than ten minutes, but for now ten or fifteen minutes of intensity is more desirable than thirty minutes of kind of doing it.

Set a timer for ten minutes that will sound when you're done so that you won't be peeking at a clock. Remember to exhale each time like it's your last breath; that's how much you should concentrate on it. It's important to relax your eyes during this meditation to avoid eye strain. If you ever see a practitioner of Zen doing this, you will notice that his or her eyes are hooded (or at about half mast). It's all about the breathing, especially the exhaling.

If you find that all of a sudden you have to take a normal breath or even pant for a couple of breaths during Zazen, that's OK. You're not breathing normally, so it will take some time to get used to this style of breathing. As soon as your breathing normalizes, go back to the practice with the normal inhaling and long slow exhaling. Don't worry; you will get it. It just takes the body a little time to adjust.

My Sufi used to say the mind is like a bull. If you lock it in a box and wave a red flag at it, you will have a problem—the bull will break free. The same is true of the mind. We don't force ourselves to concentrate on the breath by telling ourselves we can't think; instead, if we find ourselves distracted by a thought or daydream, we simply guide ourselves back to the count and the exhaling. If we are distracted by a noise, we simply guide ourselves back to the count and the breathing.

The best way to think of this is to tell yourself there are really two minds at work: One is the chatterbox who you always thought was the real you, and the other is the observer who with time and practice will become stronger than the chatterbox.

As time passes, you will develop a much deeper ability to concentrate and will learn to silence your mind. Remember—it's a journey, not a race. There are no victories in Zazen, only development. The key word here is *develop,* so don't mentally beat yourself up if at first your mind is all over the place. The brain is a reactionary organ, and the mind is its by-product, and it's only natural for it to be all over the place. Please know that as you develop, you will realize that your true nature of being is the observer and that it has always been there quietly under your chatterbox. Zazen merely frees you from the illusionary overlay that is the talking mind.

As time passes with this practice, you will notice that the time you keep the count and concentrate on breathing will become longer. Because in this style of Zazen your eyes are open, you should also be aware of your body and your surroundings. Although at first this will be hard to understand, your surroundings, your body, the wall, the noises around you, and even a stray thought are all a part of Zazen. Zazen does not isolate you from your surroundings, nor was it ever meant to. In fact, it does the opposite: It creates a state known as "Mu shim," or "No Mind." When you do not think, judge, plan, scheme, or worry, you become a part of whatever you are doing completely, so even if there is a stray thought, because you have a quiet mind, it does not tie your mind up or distract it; the stray thought merely passes through.

The state of Mu shim is highly desirable to people who have to fight to stay alive, which is why this style of Zazen was embraced by the Japanese Samurai. In a fight between two highly trained warriors, there is no time for thinking about strategy or trying to anticipate what your opponent will do. You can only rely on your training and move when your opponent moves. Anything more than that and you will die, so a Samurai with an empty mind is completely in the fight and his concentration is total.

After a month or two, if you feel that your concentration is totally there during your ten or fifteen minutes of Zazen, you may choose to move to the second phase of the practice. If you never go past the first phase, you are still doing Zazen, so please don't feel you have to go to the second phase if you don't want to. You will find that by just doing the first phase of breath counting, your concentration will improve dramatically. If you do choose to go on, the next phase is very simple.

To do the second phase of Zazen, you simply drop the mental count. In this phase, it's all about the exhaling. One of the mistakes most beginners make when concentrating on the exhaling is that they make the exhaling loud. By making the exhaling loud, you are using the exhaling like a verbal mantra. A verbal mantra is a sound repeated over and over again during meditation and is in a sense a verbal block to thought because you are hearing something besides your own mind.

My teacher warned against this style of meditation because while it will produce altered states of consciousness, it will not help you with your concentration or bring out the observer. It is simply cheating and will hinder your development.

So for ten or fifteen minutes, you are just doing a quick inhale and a slow exhale while being aware of the feeling of the breath leaving your body. There will always be a sound of the breath as you exhale, but just remember to keep it quiet. Concentrate on the breath just as you did when you were counting it. Pretend that each exhaling is the last one you will ever do. I'm going to use an old analogy here: Become one with the breath. Remember that thoughts will sometimes sneak in, but that's all right. We don't chastise ourselves for the stray thought; we simply come back to the breath. As time goes on, you will notice that stray thoughts will break in less and less often and that sometimes it will be only half a thought before the observer takes over.

Sometimes during Zazen, you will notice that you start sweating profusely. This is known as a concentration sweat. It used to happen to me all the time when I first started doing the practice. I spoke to my teacher about it, and he asked me if it was a distraction. I said that indeed it did distract me to have sweat running down my face while simply sitting in a chair and breathing.

His answer was simple and was something I've been saying ever since: Make it a part of your practice, and don't let it catch your mind. Simply concentrate on the breath and let the body do what it will do. Unlike other methods of meditation, in Zazen it's all a part of the practice. The observer is not distracted because it only observes. So if you find yourself getting wet during Zazen, don't sweat it. (Sorry! I just couldn't help myself.)

The third phase of Zazen is even simpler than the second phase. To do this phase of Zazen, you drop the breath. I don't mean that you stop breathing, but rather that you stop using the exhaling as a focal point of your concentration. After a couple of months of phase two, you will find that you can quiet your mind and simply sit without a thought entering your mind. The observer will be that strong; it will become part of your mind to such an extent that you will be able to turn it on at will.

I have done this style of Zazen, but I personally don't like it. I like to have the focal point of the breath, although I still do the third phase of Zazen on occasion just to keep things interesting. It is this state of Mu shim ("no mind") that is so prized by people like the Samurai. You will never be more "here" than you are when you are in total "no mind."

There is a word of warning I should give you: As I write how each level or refinement of Zazen gets simpler, please know it does not get easier. You can't skip ahead. Just as you have to crawl before you can walk, the same is true of Zazen. You have to give your mind more to work with in the beginning before you can concentrate through the observer or (to put it another way) with a completely silent mind. It is a process of growing and learning as well as a process of simplifying and paring away the noisy mind.

It is one worth doing, but you must be patient. When you can sit in a chair with your mind completely blank and totally in the moment, you will realize what a fantastic gift the practice of Zazen has helped you achieve, but the price for this gift is time and commitment.

Also I should warn you that with the practice you will become much more intuitive. I had been doing Zazen for about three months when I had a sudden feeling (and in fact could clearly see in my mind) an auto accident that had happened up the road from where I worked. It hit me like a sledge hammer and then it was gone, so I continued working, thinking that the incident was a figment of my imagination.

As I drove home that night, I came across the accident I had seen in my mind, and the police and fire department workers still had not managed to free the woman from the wreckage of her torn-up automobile. The accident had happened right where I saw it happen. Zazen has the ability to open up the intuitive mind. I can't really explain why this takes place, and with you maybe it won't. In Zen, they say "The master always knows," and believe me the master really does know!

The advanced Samurai would work hard to silence his mind so as to feel the intent of people around him, which was referred to as feeling the Wa. It makes it so much easier to stay alive if you know any person or persons in a crowd who intend you harm. This is one more benefit to the silent mind.

I have outlined a complete system for learning the valuable art of concentration, and all you have to do is do the work. Is Zazen necessary for the accomplishment of levitation? Not at all, but I will say this. In our present world, we are constantly interrupted. We have learned to seek entertainment as a means of staying externalized because we feel safer that way; we are constantly looking for something to do without actually concentrating on what it is we are actually doing.

But you should not approach learning levitation with a distracted mind. If you find yourself thinking about video games or your significant other or this or that, you will never be focused enough to feel the subtle energy in your body that will make levitation possible. Even if you do learn to levitate, if you can't focus your mind, how will you ever use it in a dangerous situation? The chatterbox mind will happily keep a running commentary of how much trouble you are in right until you die. You don't need that, trust me.

If you really want to be old school (as I hear the kids say nowadays), there is one more thing I should teach you: how to hold your hands during Zazen. (The truth is that if I didn't teach you this, my teacher would look me up just to hit me with a stick.) The left hand is placed in the right hand with both palms up. The right hand's fingertips should rest on the knuckles of the left hand, and the back of the left hand's fingernails should rest about midpalm of the right hand. Now bring the tips of your thumbs together to form a large circle with your two hands. Be mindful of your thumbs so that they do not form a peak or a valley. With your hands joined in a circle, place them in your lap, up against your stomach. The back of the fingers are resting in your lap, and the thumbs are up. You will see this position on several statues of the Buddha and other Eastern mystics.

What it represents is more important than the actual hand position itself. If you measure about three inches below your belly button, divide your body in thirds from the back to the front, and focus on the point one-third in from the front of your belly, you will have located the seat of vital life force in the human body. It looks like the sun on a foggy day, a pure white ball of sun-like energy that is bright but not so brilliant you can't gaze upon it easily.

There is another style of Zazen that meditates on this seat of life force. This is generally a closed-eye type of meditation and requires the practitioner to not only concentrate but visualize as well. I have read accounts from people who have mastered this style of Zazen, and they say that when they have reached full concentration and focus the sun-like ball of energy in their stomach, it looks like a fission event (some even describe it at "going into fission").

In either form of Zazen, the hands are traditionally held in the circle position in the lap to represent the sun-like seat of life force. It does not represent the circle of karma or the circle of life or anything else like that, so don't be fooled by the uninformed. But I find after doing it for years that it acts like a mental stabilizer that tells me it's time to quiet the talking mind. As far as closing off the energy in the body or anything like that, my teacher said no, that it doesn't do that.

It just tells us what we are doing and reminds us to be tuned into the seat of life force. If you're interested in the visual style of Zazen, there is a book out there called *Zen Karate* (if it's still in print) that teaches in detail this style of Zazen. I find the breathing style of Zazen more than meets my needs, and there are many Zen teachers who would agree. No matter how you do it, it's all Zazen.

I believe if you take three months to explore Zazen, you will be better off for it; however, perhaps you think this is not for you. Let me ask you this: Wouldn't it be better to learn to become wholly a part of the reality you are experiencing rather than always being slapped around by it? Think about it.

Finally, let me say this (even though my teacher will not like it because it goes against tradition): If it bothers your eyes to do the open style of this practice, you can do it with your eyes closed. You have to concentrate harder because it's just not distracting thoughts that will try to sneak in but also daydreams. This is one of the reasons the masters do it with their eyes open—their mind is not as likely to fall into the trap of visual imagery with their eyes open.

I have found as I have gotten older that doing Zazen with open eyes leaves me blurry eyed for quite a while after I have finished with the session, so I have started closing my eyes as I concentrate on the final breath. It's just one of the changes I have had to make for my aging body.

I have to laugh at myself, though, because I still hear my teacher's words when he spoke of people doing closed-eye meditations. He would get angry and exclaim, "They're not meditating; they're sleeping!" In all honesty, I am greatly indebted to my teacher for his training, but I have to say this: Make it right for you, and don't be afraid to adapt.

Finally let me teach you the two questions that you will be able to answer if you choose to meet the observer. The first question is, "where am I?" and the second question is "what time is it?" The observer will answer the first *"here"* and the second *"now"*.

With that let us continue.

THE ABILITY TO LEVITATE
(And All That It Entails)

I think the first question on everyone's mind is this: How long will it take me to achieve levitation if I choose to follow you down this path? I guess the best way I can answer that is to tell you how long it will not take you to achieve levitation. My method is not the only one out there.

In the East where they practice Chakra meditation, there are those who can and have achieved levitation. These teachers will usually tell you that the ability to levitate is assigned to a Chakra or a connecting link between the Chakras. Different teachers will assign the ability of levitation to different Chakras or their connecting energy paths.

There seems to be some disagreement as to which Chakra or connecting path between the Chakras does what exactly, but I will tell you this: All of them are high in the body, meaning a brow Chakra or a throat Chakra or the connecting links between them. The ability to levitate is never assigned to lower Chakras.

I will say it again—energy follows intent. Meditate on a point of your body like your forehead or your throat, and that's where the energy will go, to your upper body. It only follows that you will sometimes, by accident, achieve levitation with your energy pulled up your body like that. I hope you keyed in on the word "accident" because quite frankly that's what's really happening here.

Some practitioners have reported that after meditating for a period of time, they open their eyes to find themselves in a different position on the floor. Yes, that's right; they slid while meditating on a higher Chakra. It happens and is usually by accident. It can take years of practice before you have this type of accident with levitation. Sometimes it can take even longer to control levitation when you sneak up on it like this.

Chakra meditation is about spiritual development, not developing extra-normal abilities. The truth is that you can't develop just a part of your mind. Try to develop your mind in one area and those pesky extra-normal abilities have a way of sneaking up on you, so sometimes the Chakra meditation folks will levitate. I've heard that sometimes even mantra meditation practitioners have accidental levitation experiences. Go figure.

That said, let me share with you an ancient way the Kung Fu folks teach their practitioners levitation. In Kung Fu, there are several different types of Chi Kung. A Chi Kung is something a Kung Fu artist does outside of his or her normal practice to develop a special ability. For example, one Chi Kung involves picking up a large barrel in a bear hug around its middle and squeezing it with all your might for as long as you can. Each day a cup of water is added to the barrel; after the barrel is full of water, a cup of sand is then added again each day until the barrel is full. Wet sand is not light, and this Chi Kung produces a man who can kill you with just a little hug (he would be a hit at family reunions).

Other Chi Kung practices produce tremendous hand strength or finger strength, but the one I find most interesting is the Chi Kung for the development of levitation (yes, they even have one for levitation).

The practitioner first acquires a very large ceramic jar. The jar must have thick, strong walls and a large circular opening on the top, with a very small circular base on the bottom. These jars usually stand about three feet tall or more, and the opening on top is larger than a man's shoulders are wide. They have a nice round shape so that the jars would roll around rather than fall over and break. The flat base that actually contacts the ground is no more than a foot in diameter; this small base makes it so you can push these jars over with a finger. Although this may sound impractical, this instability is just what the Kung Fu practitioner is after.

After acquiring this large and unstable jar, the Kung Fu practitioner next builds a strong bamboo trellis over the jar that supports his weight and that is tall enough that while he is standing on the rim of the jar, he can reach overhead and hold onto the trellis to keep his balance. Now begins the fun part.

Standing on the rim of the jar and holding onto the overhead trellis, the practitioner positions his or her feet equally on both sides of the jar rim. Over time, both feet are moved backward or forward on the jar lip in the same direction while the practitioner learns to keep his or her balance. There's a lot of panicked grabs for the trellis at this point, let me tell you. As time goes on, the practitioner of this Chi Kung will learn to stand with both feet together on the edge of the jar lip without holding onto the trellis and without the jar falling over. How much time? Well, a gifted practitioner can do it in three years; however, it is accepted that usually this Chi Kung takes five years to master. Again it's sneaking up on levitation, and it takes a long time.

My method, on the other hand, will usually get you results within ninety days if you follow the course I have laid out for you. If you're young and healthy, you will probably have results faster than that; if you're older and unhealthy, it may take longer, but if you persist with the exercises, you also will achieve levitation.

The reason my method works so much faster than the others is that you are not sneaking up on levitation by fooling around with balance or a Chakra and the connecting links between them; you hit levitation from several angles. By that I mean you change the thought that makes and defines you with the Foundation Technique, and at the same time you make levitation a viable solution for your mind to problems you encounter in life.

You increase your available internal energy with the breath of the Magus, thus giving yourself more internal force to work with. You directly manipulate your internal energy through the vectoring exercises and the weighted exercises. Finally, I teach you how to control the chatterbox mind with Zazen so that you can get the most out of the subtle energy you're learning to control.

The ability to levitate is a lot closer than you might think. Hypnotists, in private sessions with their clients, have helped their clients achieve levitation while under hypnosis. The client and the hypnotist have to be agreeable to this type of experiment and usually be close, but believe me it does happen, usually in one or two sessions. The reason it works so quickly under hypnosis is that the person is completely relaxed and the conscious mind has taken a backseat to the subconscious mind.

The subconscious mind does not know limitations, so levitation is not a problem. Ironically, years after the levitation experience under hypnosis, many people will tell you that they don't really believe that they achieved levitation and will tell you that it was the hypnotist who made them believe they were levitating. It's amazing the lengths the mind will go when it is protecting people from things they are just not supposed to be able to do. Self-deception is just one of the many tools it uses to keep people sane and alive. This is why I implore you to use the Foundation Technique. You have to change your thought even though it's so much easier just to do the physical exercises and ignore the mental side.

By hitting the ability to levitate from so many angles, it's no wonder it comes to you so fast. As I have said before, with my method you are not sneaking up on levitation. To be honest, levitation is a weird feeling, but with the exercises I have presented in this book, you will be ready for it.

On a different note, I would like to briefly talk about jumping while just beginning to levitate. It does not work as well as you might think. The reason it does not work very well is that when you jump, you thrust the energy in your body down. In physics this is called an equal and opposite reaction. When you throw a ball, it pushes against your hand as hard as you push against it in the action of throwing it.

If you are going to try to learn levitation jumping, be aware that you really have to concentrate on keeping your energy up throughout the jump, which means keeping your viewpoint up as well. By that, I mean look up and don't make the mistake of looking down at the ground as you jump. It can be done, but levitation jumping takes a lot of practice.

It is easier to bring yourself to the point of lift and start running or walking fast and then jumping with your energy across a small stream or ditch that you might find in your path. The trick here is to push your energy forward as well as up, or you will find that you will usually stop in midair three or four feet from where you started. When I experienced levitation for the first time, I was surprised to find out that I didn't just keep going. It's not like being an astronaut in space—you don't just push off and keep going until something stops you.

Although pushing your energy up will counteract the effect gravity has on your body as far as holding you down, it will not do a thing to increase your momentum through the gravity field. Think of it this way: The distance you can jump across on the ground is about the same distance you will move while levitating, with the only change being that while you are levitating, you will stop in midair, so remember to push your energy forward as well as up.

Finally, I'm going to revisit how levitation can save your life if you find yourself stranded way up high and need to get down to ground level. This is one of the most dangerous aspects of survival levitation. Like I said earlier in this manual, if you want to learn to do this (and I do suggest you do), only do it from a height from which you will not be injured. Don't be a thrill seeker and do it from a really high place; it's totally unnecessary to endanger yourself to gain this ability.

To be honest, this is not really levitation in the classic sense. It's controlled descent, and in some cases it can be harder to master than levitation. You still push the energy up, but your intent is down. Yes, you look down as you push the energy up. It kind of goes against what I've been teaching you, but for controlled descent the rules change slightly. You also don't just jump off the high place you find yourself in.

First, you have to pull the energy up almost to the point of levitating but not quite (a good indicator that you're there is that the ground starts to feel slippery to you); then you shuffle off the edge of the place you need to get down from. Don't jump, as jumping can mess with your energy and where it is in your body. Also remember to concentrate on your energy and not on the going down part. One of the biggest mistakes you can make is to step off the edge of someplace high and forget all about your energy and where it is in your body.

A trick a Ninja would do when doing controlled descent was to open his night coat and grab the bottom edges of it in the front. He would spread his coat, and it would fill with air in the back and around the shoulders as he descended. Please know this is not enough to slow you from a fall from a high place, no matter how thin and physically fit you are!

There are several good reasons to do this. First, it keeps you upright while you descend. Remember the Ninja did their best work at night.

Survival Levitation

When doing controlled descent in the dark, you may not realize your body is not falling straight down. If you are descending at a forty-five degree angle and are pushing all your energy up through your head, you will be moving sideways through your descent. You will not be using your energy to slow your falling speed completely because it will not be working directly opposite the gravity field pulling you down, which can make for a painful or possibly fatal landing. Controlled descent only works if you are pushing the energy in the opposite direction of gravity.

Second, the Ninja did not have to waste any energy on vectoring to stay upright. The coat took care of staying upright, so the Ninja could devote all their concentration to pushing their energy up and feeling the pressure of air in the coat, which would tell them how fast they were falling in the dark. If the coat went slack or was too tight, the Ninja would adjust how hard they pushed the energy up. Vectoring was only used to change the point of landing. Controlled descent in darkness can be a sensory deprivation nightmare, and it's hard to believe a spread night coat was the solution to this potentially fatal problem.

Personally I have a terrible time with heights, and levitation did not magically cure this mental affliction as I thought it would, so controlled descent is something I have never even been tempted to do from a high place. Three feet off the ground is my limit! But having done it from that height, I know I could do it from much higher. Once you feel yourself do controlled descent, you will realize it's the same from any height.

Just be careful and don't push this training or do it from more than three or four feet off the ground. I'm not joking when I tell you that controlled descent is the most dangerous aspect of survival levitation. Only fools push survival training of any type to the point where it kills them. Please don't be that kind of fool.

I have given you everything necessary for the achievement of levitation—and a little bit more. Good luck and may your life be filled with joy and a little bit of triumphant wonder. You be safe.

The End—Or Maybe a New Beginning

ABOUT THE AUTHOR

I am a man who understands how levitation works. I gained this knowledge by trial, error, and great effort. I wish I could tell you I am a super psychic or some famous guru, but that would be a lie. I am only a man and a seeker of truth.

Made in the USA
Las Vegas, NV
23 May 2021